T0148751

WE THE PEOPLE

RETHINKING INDIA
Series editors: Aakash Singh Rathore, Mridula Mukherjee, Pushparaj Deshpande
and Syeda Hameed

OTHER BOOKS IN THE SERIES
Vision for a Nation: Paths and Perspectives
(Aakash Singh Rathore and Ashis Nandy, eds)

The Minority Conundrum: Living in Majoritarian Times
(Tanweer Fazal, ed.)

Reviving Jobs: An Agenda for Growth
(Santosh Mehrotra, ed.)

RETHINKING INDIA SERIES

WE THE PEOPLE

ESTABLISHING RIGHTS AND DEEPENING DEMOCRACY

EDITED BY

NIKHIL DEY
ARUNA ROY
RAKSHITA SWAMY

VINTAGE
An imprint of Penguin Random House

VINTAGE

USA | Canada | UK | Ireland | Australia
New Zealand | India | South Africa | China

Vintage is part of the Penguin Random House group of companies
whose addresses can be found at global.penguinrandomhouse.com

Published by Penguin Random House India Pvt. Ltd
7th Floor, Infinity Tower C, DLF Cyber City,
Gurgaon 122 002, Haryana, India

First published in Vintage by Penguin Random House India 2020

ISBN 9780670092970

Typeset in Bembo Std by Manipal Technologies Limited, Manipal
Printed at Replika Press Pvt. Ltd, India

www.penguin.co.in

Contents

Series Editors' Note

Psychologists tell us that the only *true* enemies we have are the faces looking back at us in the mirror. Today, we in India need to take a long, hard look at ourselves in the mirror. With either actual or looming crises in every branch of government, at every level, be it centre, state or local; with nearly every institution failing; with unemployment at historically high rates; with an ecosystem ready to implode; with a healthcare system in shambles; with an education system on the brink of collapse; with gender, caste and class inequities unabating; with civil society increasingly characterized by exclusion, intolerance and violence; with our own minorities living in fear; our hundreds of millions of fellow citizens in penury; and with few prospects for the innumerable youth of this nation in the face of all these increasingly intractable problems, the reflection is not sightly. Our true enemies are not external to us, not Pakistani terrorists or Bangladeshi migrants, but our own selves: our own lack of imagination, communication, cooperation and dedication towards achieving the India of our destiny and dreams.

Our Constitution, as the preamble so eloquently attests, was founded upon the fundamental values of the dignity of the individual and the unity of the nation, envisioned in relation to a radically egalitarian justice. These bedrock ideas, though perhaps especially pioneered by the likes of Jawaharlal Nehru, B.R. Ambedkar, M.K. Gandhi, Maulana Azad, Sardar Patel, Sarojini Naidu, Jagjivan Ram, R. Amrit Kaur, Rammanohar Lohia and others, had emerged as a broad consensus among the many founders of this nation, cutting across divergent social and political ideologies. Giving shape to that vision, the architects of modern India strived to ensure that each one of us is accorded equal opportunities to live with dignity and security, has equitable access to a better life, and is an equal partner in this nation's growth.

Yet, today we find these most basic constitutional principles under attack. Nearly all the public institutions that were originally created in order to fight against dominance and subservience are in the process of subversion, creating new hierarchies instead of dismantling them, generating inequities instead of ameliorating them. Government policy merely pays lip service to egalitarian considerations, while the actual administration of 'justice' and implementation of laws are in fact perpetuating precisely the opposite: illegality, criminality, corruption, bias, nepotism and injustice of every conceivable stripe. And the rapid rise of social intolerance and manifold exclusions (along the lines of gender, caste, religion, etc.) effectively whittle down and even sabotage an inclusive conception of citizenship, polity and nation.

In spite of these and all the other unmentioned but equally serious challenges posed at this moment, there are in fact new sites for sociopolitical assertion re-emerging. There are new calls arising for the reinstatement of the letter and spirit of our Constitution, not just *normatively* (where we battle things out ideologically) but also *practically* (the battle at the level of policy articulation and implementation). These calls are not simply partisan, nor are they exclusionary or zero-sum. They witness the wide participation of youth, women, the historically disadvantaged in the process of finding a new voice, minorities, members of majority communities, and progressive individuals all joining hands in solidarity.

We at the Samruddha Bharat Foundation proudly count ourselves among them. The Foundation's very raison d'être has been to take serious cognizance of India's present and future challenges, and to rise to them. Over the past two years, we have constituted numerous working groups to critically rethink social, economic and political paradigms to encourage a transformative spirit in India's polity. Over 400 of India's foremost academics, activists, professionals and policymakers across party lines have constructively engaged in this process. We have organized and assembled inputs from *jan sunwai*s (public hearings) and *jan manch*s (public platforms) that we conducted across several states, and discussed and debated these ideas with leaders of fourteen progressive political parties, in an effort to set benchmarks for a future common minimum programme. The overarching idea has been to try to breathe new life and spirit into the cold and self-serving logic of political and administrative processes, linking them to and informing them by grass-roots realities, fact-based research and social experience, and actionable social-scientific knowledge. And to do all of this with harmony and heart, with sincere emotion and national feeling.

In order to further disseminate these ideas, both to kick-start a national dialogue and to further build a consensus on them, we are bringing out this set of fourteen volumes highlighting innovative ideas that seek to deepen and further the promise of India. This is not an academic exercise; we do not merely spotlight structural problems, but also propose disruptive solutions to each of the pressing challenges that we collectively face. All the essays, though authored by top academics, technocrats, activists, intellectuals and so on, have been written purposively to be accessible to a general audience, whose creative imagination we aim to spark and whose critical feedback we intend to harness, leveraging it to further our common goals.

The inaugural volume has been specifically dedicated to our norms, to serve as a fresh reminder of our shared and shareable overlapping values and principles, collective heritage and resources. Titled *Vision for a Nation: Paths and Perspectives*, it champions a plural, inclusive, just, equitable and prosperous India, and is committed to individual dignity, which is the foundation of the unity and vibrancy of the nation.

The thirteen volumes that follow turn from the normative to the concrete. From addressing the problems faced by diverse communities—Adivasis, Dalit-Bahujans, Other Backward Classes (OBCs)—as well as women and minorities, to articulating the challenges that we face with respect to jobs and unemployment, urbanization, healthcare and a rigged economy, to scrutinizing our higher education system or institutions more broadly, each volume details some ten specific policy solutions promising to systemically treat the issue(s), transforming the problem at a lasting *structural* level, not just a superficial one. These innovative and disruptive policy solutions flow from the authors' research, knowledge and experience, but they are especially characterized by their unflinching commitment to our collective normative understanding of who we can and ought to be.

What the individual volumes aim to offer, then, are navigable road maps for how we may begin to overcome the many specific challenges that we face, guiding us towards new ways of working cooperatively to rise above our differences, heal the wounds in our communities, recalibrate our modes of governance, and revitalize our institutions. Cumulatively, however, they achieve something of even greater synergy, greater import: they reconstruct that India of our imagination, of our aspirations, the India reflected in the constitutional preamble that we all surely want to be a part of.

Let us put aside that depiction of a mirror with an enemy staring back at us. Instead, together, we help to construct a whole new set of images. One where you may look at your nation and see your individual identity and dignity reflected in it, and when you look within your individual self, you may find the pride of your nation residing there.

Aakash Singh Rathore, Mridula Mukherjee, Pushparaj Deshpande and Syeda Hameed

Introduction

Nikhil Dey, Aruna Roy and Rakshita Swamy

This book comes out at a time when countries across the world are being fundamentally affected by a tiny virus that can barely be seen under a microscope. To take on the challenge posed by COVID-19, India, like the rest of the world, will have to decide how it is going to overcome this challenging period as a cooperative exercise, where the fundamental values of equality and fraternity are strengthened, and liberty is seen not as a hindrance, but an essential aide in the path towards recovery. A policy framework that pushes people to primarily look out for themselves will only heighten and expose all our social and political weaknesses.

We could also consider this as a watershed moment, when we look towards a reordering of society, prioritize our essential principles, and face this moment with true solidarity, as equals. As almost every segment of society battles with deep uncertainties, will we recognize that in India we have perhaps the largest number of people facing the most fundamental insecurities of food, livelihood, health and the right to life? Will we use the best of what we have and strengthen it to build and redesign a new and better India? Will a rights-based framework help give people a better stake in the future? Will the Mahatma Gandhi National Rural Employment Guarantee Act (MGNREGA) become an income security programme for all Indians, like the public works programme that emerged as a part of the New Deal that the USA designed for itself to emerge from the Great Depression? Will this pandemic allow us to change the fundamentals of the economy to bring them in harmony with our constitutional values? Can this be a moment when we actually think of reversing the insurmountable trends of global warming and climate change? Can India become a more equal and compassionate society? Can access to public health and education become equal for all? Will we retain our constitutional values in the difficult days that lie ahead? Can we the people of India survive without these values? Can the biggest challenges of our nation be changed into its greatest opportunity—to truly base all policies on essential principles and values? These are important questions we need to ask ourselves as we look towards a very uncertain future.

At the time of Independence, India gave itself a constitutional democracy with a commitment to be a welfare state. 'Rights' were protected in Part III of the Constitution through the Fundamental Rights, to be enhanced through Part IV and the framework of the Directive Principles of State Policy (DPSP). The DPSP was made non-justiciable, and with that, two of the most significant kinds of dilutions got built into the framework of the state's commitment to its people. The first was the idea that even basic necessities could be an 'objective' and not a 'guarantee', built on the subjective idea of the state working 'within the limits of its economic capacity'. The second was that the state would 'strive to' minimize inequalities. The state, from its inception, was therefore not 'bound' to provide even the minimum needs for all nor ensure equity between individuals and communities.

The DPSP therefore became the agenda of action for marginalized communities and the people to realize the basic minimum needs and to strive for the principles outlined in the Preamble of the Constitution. They remain, in many ways, the crux of the dream of Gandhi's 'last man'—the millions who have lived on the fringes of the basic necessities of life, as well as the people and communities fighting for justice, including those for whom Ambedkar fought all his life.

Constitutionally, even while being non-justiciable, this set of 'objectives' should have been the framework for law and policy. It should have been the means by which poverty and destitution would be removed, and the driving force to ensure a constant constitutional challenge to inequality, injustice and exploitation.

The inequality in Indian society was one of our biggest internal challenges at birth. Ambedkar, who understood inequality in ways few others in the Constituent Assembly could, minced no words when he warned that 'inequality' would remain at the core of India's experiments with democracy and development. He reminded us that democracy is 'not a form of government, but a form of social organization'. He cautioned us to not forget the economic and the social as being intrinsic to the political. On the eve of India adopting the Constitution, which he had played such a major role in crafting, Ambedkar took his thoughts on inequality far into the future. He said, 'On the 26th of January 1950, we are going to enter into a life of contradictions. In politics we will have equality and in social and economic life we will have inequality . . . We must remove this contradiction at the earliest possible moment or else those who suffer from inequality will blow up the structure of political democracy which this Assembly has so laboriously built up.'

Just as Ambedkar looked far into the future to project the impact of these contradictions on Indian democracy, this collection of essays looks back from the other end of Ambedkar's telescope at what has happened to these contradictions, and how they have sought to be overcome. The lens for most of the authors in this volume is one of equality and justice. Therefore, while there is no attempt to ignore India's global economic position and impressive growth rate over the last couple of decades, the focus is on who has benefited most from this growth, and the struggles and movements of those who have been left out. The essays attempt to contextualize the attempts by people's movements and campaigns to secure justiciable 'rights' through law and policy in a very hostile political environment. Even though the Constitution and DPSP remained largely intact, the governing objectives were openly in contradiction of the goals of the DPSP. Even as the state reached a stage where it 'ignored' and sidestepped these objectives while formulating policy, marginalized people and communities turned to them to start advocating a rights-based framework of law and policy.

Ambedkar hoped that the eventual objective of economic democracy would be realized through the DPSP, which laid down a road map for policy. He said, 'Our object in framing the Constitution is really two-fold: (1) To lay down the form of political democracy, and (2) To lay down that our ideal is economic democracy and also to prescribe that every Government whatever is in power shall strive to bring about economic democracy. The directive principles have a great value, for they lay down that our ideal is economic democracy.'

The form and ideal that Ambedkar outlined were initially paid lip service to, then sidestepped, later diluted, and finally discredited by the new ruling elite. With the colonial masters removed and the feudal masters replaced by elected leadership, these rights should have been realized naturally and with ease over the first few years of Independence. During the first fifty years of independent India, at least the rhetoric of the government was in line with constitutional principles. The inequalities we had inherited from our feudal and colonial past continued, not being addressed through radical policy shifts or even an uncompromising determination to implement the Constitution in letter and spirit. Political parties across the spectrum understood that the vast majority of economically and socially marginalized people comprised huge voting blocks. A regular electoral system made sure that party manifestos had to pay lip service to them. However, those at the top of the economic and social hierarchy were not willing to give up power or control easily. They understood that control over social power structures and their overwhelming hold over the implementation machinery could ensure that much of the rhetoric about equity and justice would remain a mirage. They got to work on dealing with the 'form' of an electoral democracy. They understood that if they controlled the 'form', in substance they could neutralize the 'ideal'.

They succeeded to a large extent. Therefore, despite the stated intent of many elected governments of different ideological hues, promises made to most of the deprived and oppressed sections have not been met. Nevertheless, there is a limit to how long a mirage can last. Reasons for the failure to reach sections of the people continued to be examined, and it was explained that the machinery of delivery was riddled with corruption, and that those who made policy were far removed from reality. While there were certainly elements of truth in this analysis, in essence, it was another diversion.

The Indian ruling elite has proved to be quite adept in doublespeak. On the economic side, the global success of selling the capitalist project of a consumer dream influenced the spartan consumption patterns in India as well. India was also greatly influenced by trends across the world. Even the poor were fed the rhetoric that it was not redistribution that would help them but the wonders of the free market, and that 'trickle-down' theories would open up opportunities that would empower them. On the social side, those in charge were gradually mastering the art of dividing voting blocks of marginalized majorities and working to build a majoritarian identity where the social elite would be the legitimate leaders. Hindutva and neoliberal globalization were at work in parallel pathways and would come together in India in 2014. They had a common adversary—the people's demand for economic and social equality—and they sold a common dream: assertion of personal entitlement based on hierarchies, with no real need for collective reflection or control.

Those who were at the receiving end of these false dreams were not passive, but engaged in a constant struggle. People had to repeatedly call the bluff of promises, and to some it was obvious that someone else's gain was at a cost to them. The conditions of poverty and deprivation that continued to prevail also drew the subaltern and the oppressed into movements for demanding rights. These waves of popular mobilization, the strengthening and spread of Dalit movements, the demands for decentralized governance, and the constant demand of 'roti, kapda aur makaan' ensured that the voices of marginalized groups kept taking centre stage, and most governments retained at least a socialist rhetoric in economic policy. This would finally be dismantled by the wave of neoliberal globalization that swept across the world close on the heels of the collapse of the 'communist states' in the erstwhile Soviet Union and Eastern Europe.

The essays in this book essentially address the period from 1990 onwards, which followed the liberalization of the Indian economy. Prabhat Patnaik and Jayati Ghosh explain how the era of neoliberal globalization driven by the International Monetary Fund (IMF) and the World Bank directly diluted these commitments by the state, and made promises of a good life through the market. It brought the market and the corporate sector into the centre stage of policy. Most mainstream political parties progressively bought into the economic growth agenda as the only measure of development. In the pre-2004 political scenario, the language of glitter was strewn before the voters, so to speak, with the slogan 'India Shining'. However, just shiny rhetoric was not enough to entice them away from the realities of deprivation. Those at the lower ends of the caste and class hierarchy had steadily grown more politically aware of their rights and made the transition from being subjects towards asserting their constitutional rights. They could not be lured by a statement of more than roti, kapda and makaan when they did not have even that. They voted against the 'India Shining' campaign in protest against the celebration of the affluent few, to assert every citizen's right to economic and social rights and to decide on policy that should be honoured by an elected democracy.

The formation of a coalition government with significant weight of the left ensured that the left-centrist section of the Congress party also exercised influence. Election promises were taken seriously, and accountability in some manner dictated that legislative promises made to the marginalized during elections would be honoured and delivered. Such promises had been made many times before, but the working out of a National Common Minimum Programme (NCMP), the public consultation process adopted by the National Advisory Council (NAC), and the particular position and mandate of the NAC to make the NCMP a reality, combined to produce an extraordinary phase of rights-based legislation and policy. This book tries to examine the broad contours of rights-based policy and legislation, and some of them in specific detail, to analyse their impact on development and democracy in India.

The Right to Information (RTI) Act was passed in 2005, entitling citizens to access government records on demand. For the first time since the British left India, the Official Secrets Act was legally challenged. This should have been a fundamental right explicitly mentioned in the Indian Constitution. Therefore, this legislation not only helped fill a long-standing void, it also put in place enabling conditions for a more participatory form of democracy. Following a mass people's movement spanning over a decade, the government accepted in most part a legislation drafted by people's campaigns and the RTI movement, and Parliament made it clear through law that any Indian citizen would have the right to look at any document or record in custody of the government, maintained in the name of the people. The RTI actually connected economic, social and political rights, and was an apt legislation to pave the way for the others that followed. It also underscored the democratic process that connected the DPSP with the political process. The Indian RTI legislation added two important components to the international discourse on RTI, which had connected it intrinsically to the freedom of expression. The Indian movement drew from the Fundamental Rights and DPSP to emphasize its additional intrinsic connections to the right to life (Article 21) and the right to equality (Article 14).

When the National Rural Employment Guarantee Act (NREGA) was enacted approximately a month later, it was a legislation historic in timing as well as in content. The fact that India, at the time of liberalization, privatization and globalization (infamously called LPG), was willing to 'guarantee' employment at minimum wage to any rural citizen was astounding. Though this was qualified by the fact that employment was for only 100 days of work a year, and only to one person per household, nevertheless, it was a universal right for every rural household willing to use its hands to earn. It was an extraordinary commitment in comparison with policies of governments across the world which were shying away from providing even basic services such as education and health. It was a strong counter to the repeated assertions that markets would be the solution and provide everything from health and education to employment and even all-round development. Annie Raja and Rajendran Narayanan write about the potentials of and challenges faced by a path-breaking legislation such as MGNREGA in these times.

The rights-based legislations that followed in the ten-year period from 2004 to 2014 were a clear indication of a 'recognition' of the economic and social rights of the people. It was not just an electoral result or an outcome of the political equations in the government, there was also a connection being made all along with the constitutional framework and the DPSP. Article 41 of the DPSP states: 'The State shall, within the limits of its economic capacity and development, make effective provision for securing the right to work, to education and to public assistance in cases of unemployment, old age, sickness and disablement, and in other cases of undeserved want.'

The right to education was elevated to a fundamental right, and the enabling legislation was passed in the form of the Right to Education (RTE) Act. In their essay, Dipa Sinha, Srijita Majumder and Ambarish Rai reflect on the efforts to secure important health and education rights in India. A quick run-through of the legislations passed in these ten years gives us an indication that there was serious attention being paid to the creation of a political atmosphere where the elected power would look at its obligations in the light of the concerns elucidated so clearly by the framers of the Constitution. There was a declaration of public promises through the NCMP, a document of the United Progressive Alliance (UPA) and its constituents, including the support of the left parties from outside the coalition. This document itself was no small achievement, and it paved the way for dialogue, and advocacy and pressure from social groups and movements, as it was a common commitment by a coalition government that could be evaluated for 'outcomes'.

There were three broad categories of rights-based legislations that were passed in this period. One set covered democratic and participatory rights such as the right to information, the Lokpal, and the Whistleblowers Protection Act. The extraordinary success of the RTI in empowering people led to the demand for more transparency and accountability measures, but also made the government extremely wary about other legislations that might empower people to hold them to account. As a result, as Prashant Bhushan and Anjali Bharadwaj discuss in their piece on independent institutions, all legislations that set up or strengthen independent democratic institutions and enable a functional participatory democracy have either not been passed or have been passed but are being forced to remain in cold storage. These build upon the important legislative changes brought about by the constitutional amendments mandating local self-governance in rural and urban areas. Thomas Isaac and S.M. Vijayanand put forward the perspectives of the legendary People's Plan campaign in the context of decentralization.

The second category of legislations that quite uniquely created the economic and development rights of people were recognized first in the NREGA. The MGNREGA, as it was later called, was in fact a legislation that overcame budgetary constraints, as outlined in the DPSP to create a guarantee not to be inhibited by budgetary allocations. Subsequently, the Scheduled Tribes and Other Traditional Forest Dwellers (Recognition of Forest Rights) Act, 2006, called the Forest Rights Act (FRA), was passed. This was a very important legislation which for the first time since Independence 'recognized' the rights of the oldest inhabitants of this country, who were systematically being classified as encroachers on their own land. Similarly, the Street Vendors (Protection of Livelihood and Regulation of Street Vending) Act, 2014, recognized the rights and livelihoods of street vendors who only wanted the right to carry out their occupation.

The third category of legislation passed created both welfare and equality rights for particularly marginalized communities and people. The National Food Security Act (NFSA) did not really guarantee complete food security, but took a step towards guaranteeing access to affordable foodgrain to a large proportion of the population. The Unorganised Workers' Social Security Act, 2008, recognized in a minimalistic way the social security promises that needed to be made to India's vast social security sector. This was highly constrained by low budgetary allocations. The Rights of Persons with Disabilities Act, 2016 (introduced and almost passed in 2014), replaced the 1995 disability legislation passed by Parliament to bring it in consonance with the rights-based framework and the United Nations Convention on the Rights of Persons with Disabilities, which India ratified in 2007. The Protection of Women from Domestic Violence Act, 2005, was enacted to protect women from domestic violence. While N. Paul Divakar and his colleagues look at the larger means of reducing inequalities, the Scheduled Castes and the Scheduled Tribes (Prevention Of Atrocities) Amendment Act, 2015, became a powerful means of strengthening the equality and civil rights of communities affected by discrimination.

The last two Acts created civil rights for two categories of vulnerable communities—women and Scheduled Castes and Scheduled Tribes—vis-à-vis other citizens. This was to acknowledge the need to have the state play a proactive role in protecting the vulnerable from powerful people and communities. Once again, the DPSP was evoked to enable the passage of these legislations.

Did these legislations work in a country notorious for poor implementation? The experience seems to show that they worked better than schemes of the past, but the rights-based framework was also accompanied by a democratic people-based framework for governance. As the essay by Rakshita Swamy, Shankar Singh and Paras Banjara shows, even this framework of social accountability is influenced by Ambedkar's idea of social democracy and social accountability.

Constitutionally, this should have been the framework for law and policy, as defined by the DPSP. At the time that these series of laws was passed, some people felt that a new welfare and rights-based framework had come to stay. However, even the UPA had voices of contradictory intent, and the market forces in the UPA combined with others from the National Democratic Alliance (NDA) derided these policies. The market and the corporate sector had been at the centre stage of policymaking, and did not let go of its influence over the political economy, and therefore the democratic processes of governance itself.

The 2014 elections saw the coming together of market forces with the demand for Hindutva. This was a strong assertion of entitlement by those at the top of the hierarchy. The successful Hindutva formulation of a Hindu electoral majority, combined with the economic power of market and corporate forces, was an assault on the framework of rights-based legislation. The years following 2014 have steadily undermined the gains of marginalized communities from the previous decade. Power has been centralized. After an open attack on rights-based legislation, such as the MGNREGA or the Amendments to the SC/ST Prevention of Atrocities Act or the Amendments to the Land Acquisition Act, backfired on the ruling alliance, the rights-based laws have been pushed into the dark zone of laws that will neither be rescinded nor properly implemented. Some are being amended by the Centre, some by the states where the BJP is in power. Protests for their implementation are now curtailed under new draconian laws which proclaim advocates for such movements and their activities as 'unlawful activities'.

Many of the amplifiers of the voices of mass mobilization by Tribal or Dalit communities are in jail.

The story of India's democracy clearly has many more chapters to be written. Democracy seemed to have progressed from its dependence on the skeletal frame of representative democracy to evolve a structure for participation in the decade beginning 2004. With the slew of rights-based legislation enacted in India, democracy seemed to have come of age. However, the next decade will show that it is a struggle between two world views.

Where have the rights-based legislations taken us? What is looked at in isolation shows potential and promise. The RTI, the Land Acquisition amendments, the MGNREGA, etc. have been wounded by the assault on them, but will survive. In fact, in some cases, even a hostile government turns to these laws in a crisis. However, if one evaluates India against the framework of the Constitution and the DPSP, we are currently moving in an opposite direction. Article 38(2) in the DPSP says, 'The State shall, in particular, strive to minimize the inequalities in income, and endeavor to eliminate inequalities in status, facilities and opportunities, not only amongst individuals but also amongst groups of people residing in different areas or engaged in different vocations.' The essay by Amitabh Behar and Savvy Soumya Misra draws on the annual global Oxfam inequality reports to show that India is still one of the most unequal places and countries on the planet. The question of climate change and the environment has been buried under the growth rate race, whereas it is clear that inequality and the threat to the environment go hand in hand.

It has become important today—perhaps as much as it was when Europe was struggling against the crippling controls of the dark ages—to reassert the causality of the growth of civilization with rationality and, of course, ethics. The basic system which houses almost all our public life is the political economy, within a broadly coherent structure of economic, social and political democracy. Democracy now stands at the edge of an abyss, where practically all ideas and values meander in the world of semantics, couched in doublespeak, where language has been subtly co-opted and academic rigour replaced by popular jargon. We move from the universities of learning to what is known in popular idiom as 'WhatsApp University', peddling misinformation as knowledge and prejudice as axiomatic truth.

Finally, it is back to Ambedkar's questions of economic and social inequality. Those who are pushed to the boundaries of this structure and become mere digits or fingerprints are situated in a world where the reality is too strong to be denied. They stand up continually to grasp the rope of rationality for survival, to build a political economy and a public policy on which to reclaim constitutional promises for rights and for dignity, and reconstruct their livelihood and lives. Today, with multiple influences on the electoral process, even political equality is under threat. It is the struggle for economic and social equality that might provide some real alternatives. The struggle will continue, in which the rights-based framework will provide a path of inspiration and engagement for social movements for many years to come.

For a Set of Universal Economic Rights

Prabhat Patnaik and Jayati Ghosh

While the need for instituting a set of fundamental political rights is generally recognized and enshrined in all democratic Constitutions, there has scarcely been any similar recognition of the need for a set of fundamental economic rights. On the contrary, serious *theoretical* reservations have been aired on the question of the provision of such economic rights.

These reservations come from two sources. First, there is a liberal argument regarding economic rights, which contends that a right has no meaning unless the state is in a position to guarantee it. Since economic rights cannot be guaranteed by the state, as their fulfilment depends upon the capacity of the economic system, it is pointless to legislate a set of economic rights. What is the point, for instance, in enacting a right to employment if the functioning of the economy is such that it cannot be guaranteed? Economic rights, therefore, are best left un-enacted, but the ideas behind them can be used as markers for pointing to the type of society we should be aiming to build. It is perhaps such an understanding which underlies the fact that the Indian Constitution institutes a set of social and political rights but relegates what should have been economic rights to the Directive Principles of State Policy.

This argument against economic rights, however, is fundamentally flawed, since it makes democracy adjust to the limitations of capitalism, that is, it privileges a particular economic system, capitalism, above the demands of democracy. Democracy demands that the citizens of a country must have basic economic security and that this should be provided not as largesse from the state but as their due, that is, by the fact of their being citizens. It should, in other words, be provided as a matter of right. To say that we cannot have such rights because we have an economic system that cannot guarantee their realization amounts therefore to abridging democracy for the sake of preserving a particular economic system, which is a complete inversion of what should be the correct priority.

In fact, accepting this logic does not just mean prioritizing capitalism over democracy, it runs the risk of accepting the status quo in matters of economic arrangement. Whatever the economic arrangement that happens to exist in a country, whatever the specific form of capitalism that happens to prevail, no matter whether it is characterized by large-scale bribery, corruption and nepotism, the predilection of this argument would be to reconcile with that arrangement rather than to overthrow it under the compulsion of having to cater to a set of economic rights. This argument, in short, entails the privileging of the status quo.

The effective counter to this argument is that the acceptance of democracy, as mentioned earlier, should mean the provision of basic economic security, and this security should be provided through a set of economic rights. And the economic arrangement must be so altered that these economic rights are actually guaranteed. In other words, the economic arrangement must serve the needs of democracy, rather than the other way around.

The second set of objections to the institution of rights comes from the left. These go back to Marx's critique of human rights in his early essay 'On the Jewish Question', where he says, for instance, that 'the rights of man . . . are nothing but the rights of egotistic man, of man separated from other men and from the community'.[1] Human freedom, according to him, consists in overcoming alienation, and not in enjoying a set of rights as 'monads', as self-centred, isolated individuals. Of course, Marx's remarks are not made specifically with regard to economic rights, but more generally on the concept of human rights; nonetheless they are the source of scepticism on the left on the matter of rights.

Much has been written on the question of the relationship between Marxism and 'human rights'. While some have seen an irreconcilable epistemic contradiction between Marxism and the concept of 'human rights', others have argued that the emancipatory project of Marxism cannot be carried forward without some notion of rights. In fact, they argue, Marx himself had maintained that there could be no political activity without the freedom of expression and association, which therefore had to be guaranteed through the institution of appropriate rights.

Marx's remarks in his early essay are of course meant primarily to emphasize that a society of atomistic individuals, each enjoying certain rights, does not constitute true emancipation; for the latter, a new 'community' must come into being. However, there is an additional point to note in this context. Capitalism is a 'spontaneous system' which is driven by its own immanent tendencies, through the actions of individual agents who are forced by competition to act in particular ways. The atomistic individual under capitalism does not act according to his or her own volition, but is forced to act in particular ways, for otherwise he or she would fall by the wayside as a consequence of the Darwinian struggle in which capitalism traps all economic agents. 'Combinations' of workers are the first blow against this spontaneity of capitalism, and they constitute the genesis of a new 'community'.

A regime of economic rights constitutes a blow against the spontaneity of capitalism. Therefore, this regime cannot be instituted except through struggles, that is, through collective action. Hence, even though the rights may be individually enjoyed, they can come into being only through a collective struggle. The collective struggle of the workers that is needed for achieving a set of individual rights, including above all a set of economic rights, already makes the workers transcend their individualism. If they win these rights through such collective struggles, they have already moved away from being mere monads; if they do not, then that is all the more reason to carry on with the collective struggles.

Hence, while rights may not figure in the concept of emancipation that Marx had visualized, that ideal itself cannot be divorced from the struggle for rights; and the collective struggle for rights, whether or not it succeeds, is a means to get closer to the realization of that ideal.

Thus, the two kinds of arguments that may be put forward against the instituting of economic rights are both unconvincing. There is also a further point to note here. An immanent tendency of capital is to overcome all constraints that may be imposed upon its spontaneity. Hence, even if in particular circumstances capital is forced to make concessions of various kinds to the working class, its spontaneous tendency is to negate these concessions over time. Instituting a set of justiciable, universal economic rights is a means of preventing such future negation.

II

It is often suggested that there is no need for introducing any economic rights since if we maintain high GDP growth, the economic empowerment of the people would automatically get assured. But this has not happened—indeed the very opposite has taken place. Even more importantly, there is no question of its ever happening under a neoliberal regime, not even with a stepping up of the GDP growth rate.

The reason is obvious: neoliberalism entails an assault on petty production that results in arrested growth in this sector, such that per capita food production scarcely increases over time and livelihood opportunities stagnate. Since any empowerment of the mass of the working people would mean an increase in their per capita real incomes and hence an increase in their per capita demand for food, it would give rise to inflation. Inflation, however, is anathema to finance capital, which is the dominant element in a neoliberal regime, for it lowers the real value of all financial assets. The government therefore would take anti-inflationary measures involving fiscal austerity and monetary stringency, whose essential characteristic would be that they cut back on any increase in real incomes of the working people, that is, impose an income deflation upon them. It follows that a condition for the acceleration of GDP growth within a neoliberal regime is that it must not give rise to an improvement in the average per capita real income of the working people.

It may of course be argued that even if domestic food production languishes, food can always be imported, in the event of the demand for it outstripping domestic supplies, so that the above denouement need not hold. But even if the country somehow manages to find the foreign exchange required for such imports, some inflation would still be unavoidable. And to bring down such inflation, income deflationary policies would be imposed upon the working people, which would once again come in the way of their empowerment.

Therefore, to expect such empowerment to follow as a mere by-product of high growth under a neoliberal regime is a fallacy. Such empowerment has to be constitutionally mandated through the institution of economic rights, and to ensure this, an appropriate economic regime (not the spontaneously inequalizing neoliberal one which currently exists) has to be put in place.

The transition from the current regime to such an appropriate regime would no doubt be marked by difficulties, but these difficulties cannot be an excuse for keeping the working population disempowered forever. And in any case, those who argue that their condition will automatically improve under neoliberalism should not expect any serious transitional difficulties if economic rights are introduced under this regime itself.

One question that worries most people when economic rights are mentioned is that of how the resources needed for it can be mobilized. This is given more consideration in what follows.

III

Let us consider just five fundamental, universal economic rights that can be instituted: the right to food at an affordable price, the right to employment or a living wage in the absence of employment, the right to free, universal, quality healthcare through a national health service, the right to free, universal, quality education at least until the secondary stage, and the right to adequate non-contributory old-age pension and disability benefits. We will now look at the additional resources needed for instituting these rights in contemporary India.

Take the right to work. The costs of providing employment for 100 days per household to 37.5 million urban households (those living in towns with a population of less than one million) would be Rs 2.8 lakh crore per annum. This includes both wages and material costs (in the ratio 50:50), at wage rates which vary according to skill level: Rs 300 per day for the bottom 30 per cent, Rs 500 for the next 30 per cent and Rs 700 for the next 20 per cent (with the top 20 per cent assumed not to avail of such work).[2] In rural areas, if the Mahatma Gandhi National Rural Employment Guarantee Scheme (MGNREGS) actually provides 100 days of employment to every job-card holder at a wage rate of Rs 200 per day, then the total cost would be Rs 2.3 lakh crore. The two schemes together, urban and rural, add up to Rs 5.1 lakh crore. Since the current allocation for MGNREGS in the central budget is Rs 60,000 crore, the additional amount required would be Rs 4.5 lakh crore.

We have taken only 100 days of employment per household, and that too only for job-card holders in rural areas, and in towns with a population below one million in urban areas. This is not the same as ensuring a right to employment for every individual citizen, which is the aim. But there will be no more than two employment-seeking individuals per household on average (children will be in school anyway in the new situation). And the number of days of actual employment demanded, which will be in addition to the employment they already have (which would increase because of the institution of the other rights), would probably be less than 100 on average. In fact, in urban areas, it is unlikely that two individuals in 80 per cent of households would each demand 100 days of employment. Considering all these factors which act in contrary directions, we can perhaps take this figure of Rs 4.5 lakh crore as a first approximation to the amount that needs to be provided for instituting the right to employment as such.

This was a calculation made before the COVID-19 pandemic broke. The massive economic impact of the lockdown measures associated with containment has dramatically affected employment and livelihood across rural and urban areas, and the adverse effects will linger. This means that the need for such an expanded employment programme is much greater, and that more people would be seeking such employment in the medium term. Nevertheless, we retain this initial estimate of the likely costs of expansion, given that works require time to be set up and it is unlikely that expenditure in the initial years of the expanded programme would cross this amount.

Next, consider the right to food. There is already a substantial food subsidy that is provided in the budgets of the Centre and the states. The universalization of the distribution of cheap food, considering that there will be a certain amount of voluntary dropping out, would have been unlikely to require more than an additional Rs 1 lakh crore before the COVID-19 pandemic. It is now clearly much greater, given the collapse of incomes and the much greater requirement for free food access during the pandemic and lockdown periods. It is likely that providing food free or at subsidized rates to households would entail higher costs, and that this need for continued access to food would remain for a significant period. We therefore suggest a doubling of the additional amount to Rs 2 lakh crore.

As regards pensions, it has been estimated that 12.8 crore persons above the age of sixty will need to be catered to. Providing pensions, entirely on a non-contributory basis, at the rate of Rs 3000 per month to about 12.8 crore persons above the age of sixty would cost an amount of Rs 4.6 lakh crore.

On education and health, instead of making specific estimates, let us assume that 6 per cent of the GDP should be provided for the former, as suggested long ago by the Kothari Commission, from the coffers of the state.[3] This would require the state's increasing its education expenditure by 2 per cent of the GDP and its health expenditure also by 2 per cent of the GDP. These two together add up to Rs 6.6 lakh crore.

The total of all these amounts comes to Rs 17.8 lakh crore, or roughly 10.5 per cent of the current estimates of the GDP.

True, there are many expenditures we have left out; but, on the other hand, since our concern is with additional expenditure, we have not included several types of state government expenditures being incurred at present under many of these heads (of health, education, nutrition, etc.) which are quite substantial. Besides, the expenditure on some of these heads ipso facto leads to the achievement of other objectives. For instance, instituting an authentic right to education requires large-scale construction of school buildings, which also generates employment and hence serves to realize the right to employment. Adding up the requirements calculated for different heads, as we have done, therefore amounts to an overestimation. Assuming on balance that these various overestimations and underestimations cancel one another, we shall take Rs 17.8 lakh crore as the additional sum required at present for realizing these five basic economic rights.

It is also important to note that while this may seem like a large amount, many of these measures involve expenditures and expansion of public employment that typically have very strong positive multiplier effects on output. It has been found in some studies of MGNREGA that multipliers can be as high as four in local rural areas.[4] Such resulting increases in income from the initial spending would also generate more tax revenues, so that the net increase in fiscal spending would be much less. If we assume an average multiplier of two for the spending outlined above, and a relatively low average tax rate of only 15 per cent on additional incomes generated by such spending, this would mean a net increase in fiscal spending for these items of Rs 12.46 lakh crore.

How is this sum to be raised? Even if this sum is raised through taxes, that would still leave the question of real resources unresolved. In other words, raising this financial amount is not enough to prevent inflation, if not in sectors where unutilized capacity exists to begin with and where output can increase over time, then at least in food, where output increase requires specific state effort. The shock of the COVID-19 pandemic and the associated lockdown is particularly unique because it has created a simultaneous collapse of both demand and supply. In such a situation, the possibility of supply shortages emerging over time, especially for items of mass consumption, is very real, and therefore inflationary pressures are much more likely to emerge from cost-push pressures arising from specific shortages. This means that the government must undertake serious efforts to ensure continued and increased supply of essential goods and other items of mass consumption, including by recognizing the input–output relationships involved in production and distribution. Some measures would be immediate, but others necessarily require medium-term engagement, such as raising the profitability of food production, along with 'land-augmenting' measures that raise productivity per acre.

As for the financial resources, it is worth noting that in the unprecedented crisis conditions created by COVID-19, the need for the government to spend massively irrespective of the available revenues is beyond question. Therefore, the immediate increases in public expenditure could easily be covered simply by borrowing directly from the Reserve Bank of India (deficit financing, or simply money creation). In the immediate conditions of collapsing demand, such expenditure would not be inflationary, and if some of it is directed towards increasing supply (as noted above) it would reduce the supply bottlenecks that could create cost-push inflation. In addition to meeting the economic rights described above, this would also help in macroeconomic stabilization, which is an urgent necessity in a context of broad economic collapse.

Over time, the required fiscal resources can be accessed through various other means. To begin with, they have to be raised through wealth taxation, for which there is plenty of scope in India. In India, shockingly, there is virtually no wealth taxation worth the name, and wealth inequality has been increasing phenomenally. A host of economists across the world have been demanding higher wealth taxation everywhere to reverse the growing inequality under neoliberalism which they rightly see as being inimical to democracy, and even the global capitalists' own World Economic Forum summit in Davos has expressed concern over growing wealth inequality.[5] Wealth taxation in short is desirable per se, quite apart from its necessity for meeting welfare expenditures.

To be sure, any wealth taxation has to be a comprehensive one, complemented by taxes on gifts and transfers which would otherwise become instruments for evasion. But assuming that such checks are in place, wealth taxation, precisely because it hardly exists at present, can be a potent means of financial resource mobilization.

According to the Global Wealth Migration Review 2019,[6] the total net worth of private individuals in India in 2018 amounted to Rs 570 lakh crore. Of this amount, the top 1 per cent owns 58 per cent or around Rs 330 lakh crore. A 2 per cent tax on the wealth of just this stratum will fetch Rs 6.6 lakh crore per annum.

Wealth taxation has to be supplemented by inheritance taxation. As it happens, inheritance taxation is perfectly in sync with the ideology of capitalism which holds that capitalists owe their wealth to some special talent that they possess. If that is the case, then there is no reason why their children, until they too have displayed such talent, should also be the possessors of such wealth.

If we assume that every year 5 per cent of the total wealth of this top stratum gets transferred to their children, or other legatees, as inheritance, then even a modest taxation of one-third on such inheritance would fetch Rs 5.5 lakh crore. Just these two taxes, in short, and that too levied only on the top 1 per cent, would be quite enough to fetch more than Rs 12 lakh crore. This amounts to approximately the same net requirement we have estimated for the state's obligation to fulfil the five economic rights we have mentioned.

IV

Two political questions may be raised here. First, if economic rights could not be introduced at the time of framing the Constitution because of opposition from certain groups, then is there any reason to believe that things have changed since that time? The answer lies in the fact that we now have a history of seven decades to go by, which has clearly shown that the expectations entertained then about the prospects of economic betterment of the masses through 'development' have been belied. These seven decades have been a learning experience not only for the political formations that would otherwise have supported economic rights but had then acquiesced in their non-inclusion, but also above all for the people themselves, whose desire for material improvement is palpable. This desire is now being articulated through 'identity politics', demanding reservations for particular groups, but it could be channelled to better effect by demanding universal economic rights. Furthermore, the unprecedented crisis caused by the pandemic and the lockdown have created both a clear necessity for the state to meet its obligations with regards to these rights, and greater public awareness of the costs of not meeting them. This can therefore provide an opportune moment in which to rethink the social contract between people and the state in ways that would ensure the future realization of these basic rights.

A second related question is that any constitutional change in this direction requires a major effort which would be difficult to make in sheer practical terms. There could, however, be a shortcut. As in the case of the MGNREGS, a unanimous resolution passed in both houses of Parliament could de facto set up a right, even though there is no formal constitutional amendment. Since such a scheme would be fully financed by the revenue mobilized by the central government, which would be based on wealth taxation, the consent of the states would be unnecessary; and no state would dare not implement such a scheme, when it does not have to bear any additional financial burden, for fear of alienating public opinion.

It is true that the MGNREGS itself has been allowed to get whittled down over time, and is no longer, for all practical purposes, a rights-based programme. But this is because the running down of this programme by successive governments, which has clearly been in violation of the law, has not been sufficiently challenged in courts. Rights have meaning only if they are justiciable; their justiciability has meaning only if the judiciary is brought into the picture when they are violated. Of course, the judiciary being in the picture does not ipso facto guarantee the realization of a right, as is being seen today alas with regard to a host of political rights. The defence of rights requires not only social mobilization and public intervention, but also sensitivity on the part of the judiciary.

Fighting Inequality: Rights and Entitlements

Amitabh Behar and Savvy Soumya Misra[1]

Oxfam released its 2019 inequality report titled *Public Good or Private Wealth?* during the World Economic Forum at Davos. The report was downloaded more than 20,000 times in just a matter of a few days and it set the newsroom agenda across the globe for almost one full week. In India, the report was received with significant interest and attention. Growing inequality is increasingly being recognized as one of the biggest challenges of contemporary times. Even a voice like Manmohan Singh, considered the architect of pro-market liberalization in India, advised focused attention on the question of inequality. While releasing *India: Social Development Report 2018— Rising Inequalities in India*, prepared by the Council for Social Development, Singh said that India was one of the world's fastest-growing large economies but the high growth was also associated with rising economic, social, regional as well as rural and urban inequalities where some social groups and regions have seriously lagged behind. He said, 'Rising inequality should concern us all because the adverse effects of economic and political inequality can impact our march towards inclusive and sustainable growth.'[2]

Dramatic Rise in Inequality

The fulcrum of the Oxfam report is the trend of growing inequality in the world, which is reflected in the tremendous concentration of wealth amongst a few individuals and a small number of TNCs (transnational corporations). The report says that twenty-six individuals (not surprisingly, all men) have more wealth than the bottom 50 per cent of the global population. Globally, the number of billionaires has doubled since the financial crisis. India has added eighteen new billionaires in the last year, raising the number of billionaires in the country to 119. In 2018, the total wealth of India increased by $151 billion (Rs 10,591 billion). However, the wealth of the top 1 per cent increased by 39 per cent, whereas the wealth of the bottom 50 per cent increased by a dismal 3 per cent.[3]

The Global Policy Forum report by Sarah Anderson and John Cavanagh says that of the 100 largest economies in the world, fifty-one are corporations and only forty-nine are countries. Walmart—the number twelve corporation in the world—is bigger than 161 countries, including Israel, Poland and Greece.[4] According to the Oxfam report, this concentration of wealth is even higher in India, with nine men owning more wealth than 50 per cent of the Indian population, which would be roughly around 650 million people.[5]

All this data reflects that inequality is growing dramatically to obscene and frightening levels. In the last few years, more and more researchers have focused on inequality, evaluating not just its extent but also its dimensions. This academic push has not happened in a void. Across the world, inequality has risen to almost intolerable levels, and this has caused social unrest and brought about political upheavals. The fact is that the bulk of the underprivileged population of the world live in new emerging economies such as India. Indeed, several international institutions such as the World Bank, IMF and the Asian Development Bank have repeatedly raised the flag on inequality in these countries. This has led to the unprecedented step of including inequality as a global goal within the framework of the Sustainable Development Goals (SDGs). The inclusion of a politically explosive concept such as inequality in the SDGs, in spite of the sanitized nature of the global compact, is an acknowledgement of the criticality of inequality in any discussion on the future of Earth and humanity.

Understanding Inequality in India

Even so, most of the mainstream discussion on inequality has largely ignored the status of inequality in emerging countries such as India. This is partly due to the lack of adequate and comparable long-term data. For instance, many of the developing economies do not have time-series data on personal tax, incomes and wealth, and without these it is difficult to analyse the nature, extent and growth of inequalities.

In this regard, it is pertinent to note what Oxfam India's *India Inequality Report 2018: Widening Gaps* stated: 'A general misconception around inequality in India is that the level of inequality is low by international standards. However, such a comparison is largely misplaced as inequality in India is usually measured by the consumption expenditure data, which is not comparable to inequality in most countries, which is measured by income dimension.'[6]

The report further explained that while there is no one-to-one correspondence between income and consumption inequality, evidence across countries suggests that consumption inequality is generally lower than income inequality. And it is also partly because many of these countries have varied social and economic systems in place. For instance, inequality brought about by differences in caste is quite significant in India but this may not find a parallel in most developed countries, and it may not be easy to model or understand its impact if one limits the scope to research done in the developed world.

This inequality is underscored by studies that focus on India. Recent evidence on various dimensions of inequality has confirmed that India is not only among countries with high inequality but has also seen inequality increase in the last two decades.[7] The Gini wealth coefficient in India has gone up from 81.2 per cent in 2008 to 85.4 per cent in 2018, which shows that inequality has risen.[8]

According to the *India Inequality Report 2018*, India is home to 17 per cent of the world's population; it is also home to the largest number of people living below the World Bank's international poverty line measure of $1.90 per day. Given the sheer size of the population and the absolute numbers of the poor, India is a key player in world development and inequality trends. And barring a few blips, it continues to remain one of the fastest growing economies in the world. While the growth rate of the Indian economy has been slow for most years since Independence, it took off in the early 2000s. The spectacular growth post 2003–04 was also accompanied by a drastic fall in the poverty headcount ratio. However, a reduction in poverty is not the same as a reduction in inequality.

Inequality in India: Looking Beyond the Economic Dimension

As mentioned earlier, inequality in India takes more shapes and forms than in a developed country. Inequality is not limited to just the differences in wealth and income, it also shows up in the form of poorer access to basic healthcare and education facilities as well as fewer opportunities in the employment market. The *India Inequality Report 2018* states that beyond the widening economic inequalities, 'there has been marginalization and exclusion of individuals, communities, and religious groups'.[9]

Inequality leads to uneven developmental outcomes; this makes inequality unacceptable from a framework of basic human rights and entitlements. A more nuanced view could see inequality leading to a dilution of the fundamental social contract itself. For instance, it is heartbreaking to read that 42 per cent of Adivasi children are malnourished, which is 1.5 times higher than in the case of non-tribal children. Children from poor families in India are three times more likely to die before their first birthday compared to children from rich families. A Dalit woman is more likely to live almost 14.6 years less than one from a high-caste family.[10]

Underscoring Social Inequalities

In the chapter titled 'Grip of Inequality', in the 2013 book *An Uncertain Glory: India and Its Contradictions*, economists Jean Drèze and Amartya Sen state that inequality may be rising in the last couple of decades but India has a historical legacy for multiple social inequalities. It has a toxic mix of extreme inequalities— on the one hand, there are major disparities of caste, class and gender, and on the other, there is economic inequality. The latter is a manifestation of the former, which continues to have a stranglehold on Indian society.[11]

On the social side, Dalits and Adivasis have historically suffered marginalization, exclusion and exploitation. In very real terms, this has adversely affected not just their access to basic welfare and public services but also kept them from improving their health and nutrition as well as education.

In their book, Drèze and Sen show how caste hierarchies have bred inequality. They look at a 1901 study[12] that compared the literacy rates of Brahmins and Dalits. The study showed that in most regions, a majority of Brahmin men were already literate (in Baroda, up to 73 per cent). At the other end of the spectrum was the literacy rate among Dalit women, which was zero in most states. Dalit men achieved a literacy rate of at the most 1 per cent and Brahmin women a maximum of 6 per cent. The data showed a clear gender and caste monopoly of education back then.[13]

Of course, this was more than a century ago, and over the decades, India has made considerable progress. For instance, there have been improvements in the literacy rate; in 2011, the literacy rate was 73 per cent, which was higher than the 2001 data of 65 per cent. Yet, unacceptable levels of disparities are prevalent even today. For instance, Dalits and Adivasis continue to lag behind on literacy rates. Again, the worst numbers are for Adivasi women—only one of every two is unlettered.

The sad truth is that even though caste-based discrimination has been barred by law, it continues to hold sway over how India's society functions. A glaring example is the fact that Dalits continue to be employed as manual scavengers, despite it being banned by the Indian government. That social institutions play a massive role in opting for decent employment is evident from the fact that manual scavengers are rarely able to move out and get employment elsewhere. The stigma sticks to them and keeps them from improving their stead.

Again, thanks to the widening inequality, even fast economic growth hasn't really levelled out the playing field that has historically been in favour of the dominant classes. A 2011 study by Sukhadeo Thorat and Nidhi Sabharwal finds that through the 1990s and the early 2000s, the underweight prevalence among women and children, and child mortality rates of SCs and STs were higher.[14] Most importantly, as the *India Inequality Report 2018* concludes, although there have been improvements in the health outcomes across groups over the last decade, the disparity between social groups has hardly changed. A case in point is the data on child stunting—that is, children whose heights are considered lesser than normal—which shows that that the gap between SCs/STs and the rest has remained unchanged.[15] In other words, the disadvantaged groups have continued to lag behind.

Gender and the Burden of Intersectional Inequality

Oxfam India's latest report on the state of employment in India points out how 'gender as a social institution keeps women away from accessing equal wages and restricts them to occupations with casual contracts and "wages bordering on starvation".[16] Dalit women face double the discrimination due to gender and caste hierarchy and are forced to take up unclean occupations. In urban areas, it is not uncommon to find that Brahmin or high-caste women are preferred for cooking and kitchen work, and lower-caste Dalit or Muslim women are preferred for other domestic work such as washing clothes, cleaning vessels and mopping floors and toilets.[17] It clearly suggests that notions of purity and pollution which are central to the caste system are very much at work in shaping labour markets. Given the barriers, it is not surprising to find a large number of Dalit women in manual scavenging and sanitation work, which are the most stigmatized occupations.'[18]

While these instances show the huge caste disparities on the one hand, they also underscore the glaring gender gaps in India. Gender inequality has been exceptionally high in India, especially in the northern and western parts of the country.[19] Women in India have always been dealt an unfair hand; the disparities set in from the time they are born, and can be seen in the education they receive and the economic opportunities that they can explore, with violence against women restricting their mobility. If they do happen to beat all social hurdles and make it to the workplace, they get paid much less than their male counterparts.

In 2018, India was 125th (out of 188) on the Gender Inequality Index of the United Nations Development Programme (UNDP). Similarly, it ranked 108th (out of 144) on the World Economic Forum's Global Gender Gap Index—ten notches below where it stood in 2006. Indeed, it scored the third lowest in health. Its overall performance is far below the global average and behind its neighbours. 'The declining female labor force participation rate, along with the gender wage-gap and unequal access to decent employment opportunities, has exacerbated the economic and social disparity on gender lines,' as per information in the *India Inequality Report 2018*.[20] Clearly, with such gender gaps, it is hard to argue that India's growth story has been truly inclusive.

Further compounding the issue is the influence of social and religious groups. Women among SCs and STs as well as Muslims have the worst record on healthcare and educational parameters.

Religious Exclusion Exacerbating Inequality

Broadly speaking, religious identity has been seen to play a crucial role in an individual's access to basic services, mobility and human development outcomes. A high-level committee constituted by Prime Minister Manmohan Singh in 2006 and led by Justice Rajinder Sachar highlighted the various ways in which religious minorities suffered exclusion. The situation was found to be worst for Muslims even though they are the second-largest religious group by population in the country after Hindus.

The stereotyping of individuals based on religious affiliation has often led to their exclusion. For instance, stories of Muslim families not being able to rent a house in certain localities crop up with alarming regularity.

India's Muslim community has for long faced discrimination and relatively lower living standards.[21] The Sachar Committee pointed out that nearly one-third of small villages with high concentrations of Muslims did not have any educational institutions and that about 40 per cent of large villages with a substantial Muslim concentration did not have any medical facilities.[22]

Research has shown that the Muslim community has the lowest rate of enrolment in higher education in India, accounting for just 4.4 per cent of students. It also faces high levels of poverty, with 25 per cent of India's 3,70,000 beggars being Muslim.[23] Over the years, while there has been a substantial rise in the upward mobility of Dalits and Adivasis, there has been a substantial decline in the same for Muslims. In fact, access to high school and college for Muslims from the bottom half families has stagnated for the last fifteen years. This has been primarily because Dalits and Adivasis have access to reserved seats in educational institutions and jobs as opposed to Muslims.

In recent years, in addition to the discrimination faced by them, Muslims have also become targets of violence. This is further going to limit their mobility and have a more serious impact on the community's growth and development.

Why Is Inequality Growing?

The *India Inequality Report 2018* identifies the nature of economic policies since the 1990s that have allowed a greater role to the private sector in almost all spheres, including in the provision of basic services, as one of the fundamental causes of growing inequality. The report says, 'On the one hand, the consequence of the withdrawal of the state from the essential role of providing basic services which shape economic outcomes has resulted in the erosion of the state as an instrument of "inclusion". On the other hand, the nature of economic policies followed since the early 1990s also strengthened the claim of the state being a silent facilitator in rising inequality in recent decades.'[24]

Rampant crony capitalism and preferential treatment of the rich 'at the cost of the poor, and the inability of the state to protect the rights of the poor and marginalised'[25] further fuelled the gap between the rich and poor. Crony capitalism is essentially a system where businesses keep expanding their influence and wealth not by following the fair rule of the market but by benefiting from their proximity with the decision makers in the government. Thus, the distribution of licences, permits, contracts and tax breaks are all part of crony capitalism.

Over the past decade, India saw several instances, such as the 2G allocation, or coal block allocations, where state-related favours led to the rich getting richer. In other words, the richest businesses not only received favours from the government but were also supplied easy institutional credit to fund their expenditure. 'A look at the non-performing assets of the public sector banks has clearly established that the majority of these companies are held by the richest Indians,' the report says.[26] This explains the fact that 60 per cent of billionaire wealth comes from rent-thick sectors (those where income generation requires natural resources or depends on the state for licences).

In this context of crony capitalism and growing concentration of wealth, India runs a grave risk of disappointing its aspirational class of educated young people from small towns and other geographies, resulting in serious social anger and unrest.

Fighting Inequality: Strengthening Peoples' Rights and Entitlements

The *India Inequality Report* (2018 and 2019) found that not only did inequality remain high and on an increasing trend in India, there had not been commensurate efforts to reduce it. In 2017, Oxfam International and Development Finance International developed a Commitment to Reducing Inequality Index (CRI Index) to measure the commitment of governments towards reducing inequality. In 2017, India ranked 132 out of 152 countries, which was reflected in its poor commitment to the reduction of inequality; it fared worse in 2018—being placed at 147 out of 157 countries.[27]

The Oxfam report says that such extreme levels of inequality are not inevitable. Some of the top market economies of the world, such as Switzerland and even the USA, have managed it better, by taxing property and wealth (including inheritance and gift taxes) at 1.56 per cent and 2.79 per cent of GDP respectively. In contrast, India has taxed approximately only 0.8 per cent of GDP. This shows in their level of investment in essential services such as health and education: Switzerland spends 16 per cent on education and nearly 23 per cent on health as percentage of total spending. The USA spends 16 per cent and 24 per cent on education and health respectively as percentage of total spending. In contrast, the figures are stark in India. We spend 11.59 per cent on education and a mere 4.58 per cent on health as percentage of total spending. In tangible terms, India spends Rs 1112 per person on public health per capita every year. This is less than the cost of a single consultation at the country's top private hospitals or roughly the cost of a pizza at many restaurants.[28]

From a public policy perspective, it is clear that fast economic growth cannot reduce inequalities even when it does reduce poverty. Bridging inequalities requires direct intervention by the government. In this regard, the rights-based approach adopted by the UPA government under Manmohan Singh is creditable. The National Food Security Act, the Mahatma Gandhi National Rural Employment Guarantee Act, the Right to Education Act and the Forest Rights Act have been standout legislations and they have aimed at shoring up social protections for the disadvantaged lot in India. During the release of *India: Social Development Report 2018—Rising Inequalities in India*, Singh said, 'Positive government intervention to reduce social and economic inequality has to be the main theme of modern policymaking.'[29]

Himanshu and Abhijit Sen estimate that the transfers on just food-related schemes have contributed to a one-third reduction in the poverty headcount ratio and almost half of the total poverty reduction using the squared poverty gap measure. Similarly, the expenditure on MGNREGA as well as the increase in minimum support prices for various agriculture produce in the country improved the wages earned by the rural poor between 2008–13, and helped them tide over the high food inflation. These interventions also contributed to the moderation in the rising trend of inequality. From this standpoint, it is also noteworthy that many of these schemes have seen a reversal in their funding over the past few years, and this has affected the state of social protections and their impact on alleviating inequality.[30]

Given the high levels of inequalities in India, as well as the country's ability to grow fast, there is a certain menu of policies that must be adhered to if we are serious about reducing inequality. This includes progressive taxation, redistribution of assets and incomes, and public provisioning of essential goods and services such as healthcare and education. Far too often, in the Indian context, such social welfare programmes are accused of increasing the fiscal deficit. But reducing inequalities is a social necessity and a constitutional imperative for the government. India does not need piecemeal solutions, rather it needs to reconsider the structural aspect of its economic growth and its government's inability to fill the gaps.

Fighting Inequality: Moral Imperative of Contemporary Times

In the absence of timely action on reducing inequality, India will risk its ability to grow fast and remain a peaceful society. Violent protests by one social group after another in the country—often demanding government job reservations—is a pointer to the deep dissatisfaction among the people with the state of governance and their own well-being. Inequality has deep negative impacts on solidarities within the community, levels of trust and the psychological well-being of individuals. Democratic theory is full of work on how inequality and concentration of wealth in neoliberal contexts leads to crony capitalism, which distorts democracy and limits decision-making in the hands of a few.

The Indian and global leadership needs to engage and confront the moral dilemmas these levels of inequality pose to the society and world. Evading the central question of inequality by shying away from interrogating the moral, social and political dimensions of growing inequality in the name of methodological loopholes or by substituting (conveniently interchanging) inequality with poverty is irresponsible and misleading. Inequality is not merely a-contextual economic data, it is about how power distribution is skewed and how power is concentrated with a few within societies, whereas just and even distribution of power is central to a healthy society, democracy and nation.

The human project is not devoid of a moral framework; in fact, history teaches us that a moral compass built around notions of justice, dignity and equality is central to human progress. The entire moral edifice of a society collapses if it does not confront the question of inequality and human indignity. We must stand up to one of the biggest challenges of our times and respond decisively.

From Social Democracy to Social Accountability

Paras Banjara, Rakshita Swamy and Shankar Singh

Caste and class remain dominant defining features of Indian society. Its structure is built on the basis of social inequality, most often strengthened and reinforced by economic inequality. Post the era of economic globalization, the socio-economic structure resembles a pyramid, with a tiny number of people at the top cornering the bulk of resources. This would make no sense when seen as the end result of an electoral democracy, where elections are to mandate 'rule by the people'. The pyramid should actually be reversed.

It takes concerted effort to understand how in a parliamentary democracy vast majorities end up at the bottom of the pyramid. The fact that a select few at the top continue to dominate the masses, who are unable to topple them or shake the structure, points to a successful and perverted domination of the electoral process. As India laid the foundation of its political democracy, B.R. Ambedkar, considered the leading architect of the Indian Constitution, had warned us in 1949 of the consequences of deluding ourselves to believe that the political equality of 'one person, one vote' could on its own address social and economic equality. It has in fact become clear in independent India that caste and class have found a way of managing the electoral process—in such a way that even if there is 'political change' in the government, the economic, social and political domination of class and caste continue.

Electoral politics has found a way to separate the rhetoric of equality from its true implementation. Even voters are not under the illusion that their vote can change their oppression and inequality. This helps explain why there is a popular perception that there is no accountability in India. In fact, well worked-out systems of accountability exist, and continue to be exercised; it is only that they are systems that answer upwards, to those who rule, thereby perpetuating existing power structures in their implementation as well. There is no doubt that Ambedkar's view of social democracy is even more important when it comes to the question of democratic accountability.

The Relevance of Social Accountability

Ambedkar made it clear in his speech on 26 November 1949:

> We must not be content with mere political democracy. We must make our political democracy a social democracy as well. Political democracy cannot last unless there lies at the base of it social democracy. What does social democracy mean? It means a way of life which recognizes liberty, equality and fraternity as the principles of life. These principles of liberty, equality and fraternity are not to be treated as separate items in a trinity. They form a union of trinity in the sense that to divorce one from the other is to defeat the very purpose

of democracy. Liberty cannot be divorced from equality, equality cannot be divorced from liberty. Nor can liberty and equality be divorced from fraternity. Without equality, liberty would produce the supremacy of the few over the many. Equality without liberty would kill individual initiative. Without fraternity, liberty and equality could not become a natural course of things. It would require a constable to enforce them.[1]

His words of caution expose the abnormality that we face today. Why has the current form of Indian democracy perpetuated perversions of democratic practice—centralization of power and economic resources; openly targeting and spreading insecurities amongst minority communities; building vulnerabilities; polarizing people and voters; and alienating marginalized communities? While the clutches of social power structures are so firm, engrained and pervasive, and when social norms around birth, marriage and even death rituals are governed by hierarchy, how can we possibly envision a world where accountability manifests not only legally but also in terms of norms of behaviour?

It is impossible to try and craft the elements of 'social accountability' without taking into account the entrenched and sophisticated structures of social and economic inequality that determine all relationships. As long as the democracy we claim to live within does not actively recognize equality, liberty and fraternity as indispensable tenets and makes them meaningful to all those fighting to realize these rights, electoral democracy will be manipulated by the powerful to perpetuate their control. The recognition of these values does not come from a written Constitution alone. Fostering these values requires an active effort to dismantle the control of groups who hold power, by creating platforms where they are held accountable to the people. That is a bottom-up search for social accountability, of which India's Right to Information movement has been an outstanding example.

Those who come to power politically know how to navigate and use existing social and economic inequalities such that they retain exclusive control. Twenty-six individuals globally have more wealth than the bottom 50 per cent of the global population.[2] To retain their grossly unequal share of finite resources, those at the top cannot afford to have their means of control questioned and exposed. This is why discrimination, exclusion and suppression of dissent is practised and even legitimized within a system designed to protect the status quo. Growth rates, and not the distribution of the fruits of growth, are considered axiomatic signs of progress. The market and its norms are used to justify the accumulation of wealth, and elections are presented as a foolproof method of enforcing political accountability.

If we indeed want to prevent this perversion of democracy, we need to strive towards making democracy accessible to all, and on an ongoing basis. Social accountability therein plays an indispensable role. Given life through platforms, mechanisms and processes, social accountability disturbs power imbalances in favour of the weak, whether socially, economically or politically. In fact, the very conceptualization of democracy is incomplete without social accountability. If the relationship between the state and its citizens is seen in the form of a social contract, social accountability is its currency. When those who are subject to the oppression of a system—however democratic it is politically—are not able to access their entitlement, have their voice registered or their grievances redressed, their faith in the structure that governs their engagement with the state fades away, their trust erodes. The breaking of this trust is a blow to democracy in the most fundamental sense. Not having the right to exercise power to change their social reality beyond a mere vote, people begin to lose faith in democracy. When social accountability actually manifests, people begin to have faith in the system and in their own capacity to influence decisions. This does not arise immediately on account of systemic corrections happening miraculously because of peoples' assertions. The battle is long and fraught with non-linear progress. But the ability to know, question, articulate their disagreement and have their grievances redressed results in people identifying and acknowledging their own relevance in a democracy. The faith of the most marginalized and the most oppressed in the nature of the state to stand by the Constitution is what keeps democracy alive and legitimate.

A Framework of Social Accountability[3]

A slogan that was a part of the early days of the Right to Information movement in Rajasthan was: 'Democracy is transparency, with accountability to the people.' Social accountability can be defined as the flow of accountability from the state to its citizens and can be understood as a progression from transparency to accountability to the people. A structured regime of social accountability establishes the right of citizens to know the how and why of decisions, their implementation and their results with the power to influence policy formulation.

By their very nature, social accountability theories draw from practice. However, the academic discourse on the subject is dominated by the articulation of its intrinsic elements and components by theorists and academicians. Moreover, the discipline is perceived in practical terms, more often than not, as a discourse on 'techniques' and 'tools' rather than one on long-standing issues of power and inequity.

The lack of accountability is felt most acutely by ordinary citizens, particularly the most vulnerable and marginalized, in their daily engagement with the state. It takes the form and shape of violation of rights, denial of access, discrimination, deliberate exclusion and democratic marginalization. Therefore, for a definition of social accountability to be meaningful, it should ideally be framed by the people facing the lack of it the most. A group of Dalit students from Bhilwara district in Rajasthan articulated one such conceptualization of social accountability, based on their lived realities. Talking to Mazdoor Kisan Shakti Sangathan (MKSS) activists about the principles of an 'accountability to the people' law, they said that people needed: (a) actionable information (*jankari*); (b) a dated acknowledgement for every complaint (*sunwai*); (c) a speaking order within a fixed time frame (*karyawahi*); (d) participation (*bhagidari*); (e) protection to the complainant (*suraksha*); and (f) a collective official platform for redress (*janta ka manch*). And that is how the 'Bhilwara Principles of Social Accountability' were first theorized. These principles have now even been acknowledged by the Comptroller and Auditor General as the 'minimum principles' of the Auditing Standards of Social Audit. They conceptualized six elements intrinsic to social accountability:

Actionable information: Information is power. People need information to know, act, self-govern, make informed choices and hold those who govern accountable to their mandate. Access to information that is credible and comprehensible is therefore an essential element of democracy in action. Having the relevant information, having a widespread understanding of the entitlements, of the prescribed time frames, of who is responsible for what, of the prescribed standards and rates, of the decision-making processes, of the possibility for appeal, complaint or grievance redressal, and of the reasonably expected outputs and outcomes is the first element of social accountability.

Hearing with a dated acknowledgement: For a system to facilitate accountability, there must be adequate, inclusive and multiple modes for citizens to articulate their grievances, for reporting any of the ways in which their rights are violated. And each time a citizen reports a grievance, it must be acknowledged. Certain categories of people such as the elderly, children, the illiterate and single women will need more sensitive facilitation in order to register and track their grievances. This forms the second element of social accountability.

Time-bound action: Going beyond the articulation of a grievance and its due acknowledgement, citizens need to have a guarantee of their complaints being redressed within a fixed time frame. And if this is not done, they have the right to be compensated for the same. This forms the third element of social accountability.

Participation of all concerned: Participation of a citizen in the process of his/her grievance being redressed through institutionalized platforms forms the fourth element of social accountability. Participation plays a central role in enabling the voice of communities to reach the state while accessing services, planning for the use of public funds, monitoring programme delivery and registering grievances. Through participation, citizens can claim fair allocation of resources, bring to notice instances of fraud and misappropriation, and demand retribution and restoration. However, for participation to reach these objectives, it must be institutionalized. Otherwise, only some sections of the community will be consulted, and this will then be taken as feedback from the entire community, which will not be true.

Institutionalized democratic peoples' platform: To enable meaningful interaction between the citizens and the state, there must be a platform for the former to publicly and collectively engage with the latter. This forms the fifth element of social accountability. Such platforms enable citizens to dialogue with the state on a more equal footing, and give a chance to sharpen the spirit of public inquiry for the development of a critical awareness of collective social realities. It facilitates the citizen's 'truth' to stand a chance against the official record, when they are different.

Protection: With such elements of social accountability in motion, vested interests do not fall short of methods to suppress and intimidate those who reveal the nexus of power that perpetuates corruption. The protection of citizens, particularly whistleblowers, who enable the unearthing of social, political and financial corruption through information is therefore of immense significance and forms the sixth and last element of social accountability.

Explorations in Social Accountability

When the system begins to share information and gives citizens, individually and collectively, a platform to articulate their grievances in their own language, and also takes time-bound corrective action on grievances, not only do people start exercising their rights through the system, they also start exercising their duty of citizenship, using public and community monitoring to make everyone accountable to each other. Accountability becomes a two-way process.

MGNREGA

The Mahatma Gandhi National Rural Employment Guarantee Act is an example of a rights-based law that not only built accountability into different entitlements—unemployment allowance if work was not provided in fifteen days; compensation if wages were not paid in fifteen days, etc.—but also provided a generic model of statutory social accountability, that is, social audits, to make the entire law subject to processes of social accountability. It has shown that a rights-based framework in itself cannot guarantee outcomes unless that pursuit is enabled by enforced mechanisms for citizens in seeking accountability. By heralding the rights-based paradigm of development in the social sector, the passage of the MGNREGA also pioneered the democratic reform of institutionalizing social audits and mandatory disclosure of information in the public domain. Stated as a single-line provision in the law in 2006, social audits have transformed into a legitimately accepted means of public oversight in governance through a decade-long process that involved the notification of rules, and the development of Auditing Standards of Social Audit by the Comptroller and Auditor General's office (becoming the first such instance of a supreme audit institution developing standards for social audit anywhere in the country) and the expansion of its scope by the Supreme Court through numerous judgments.

Shiksha Samwaad

Education is essential to a strong development framework, which requires the joint efforts of all segments of society. A well-functioning school is the outcome of collaborations between many stakeholders: teachers, students, parents, school management committees, principals, the administration and elected representatives. These stakeholders do not have a common platform on which they come together and have a collective dialogue. In the absence of such a platform, there is a tendency for one entity to keep blaming the other as a means of absolving themselves of their primary duty with respect to ensuring that the school functions as per the legal mandate.

Shiksha samwaads (education dialogues) were initiated in the Kumbhalgarh block of Rajsamand district, Rajasthan, in collaboration with civil society organizations (national and local)[4] and the Department of Education to confront this problem. An informed dialogue then took place—issues were raised, discussions happened, solutions emerged and responsibilities were divided. The spirit of democratic dialogue actually surfaced and people had to push themselves to arrive at decisions. They could not rest only within binary choices. Multiple examples emerged of how such a routine dialogue resulted in arriving at conclusive action across a range of grievances, such as deployment of additional teachers and using the help of volunteer teachers on a temporary basis, parents doing voluntary labour to complete the construction of partial compound walls, getting dedicated water and electricity supply assured to the schools, amongst many other things.

Building and Other Construction Workers Act

Recognizing the need for implementation of such an essential piece of legislation to meet the highest standards of efficiency, inclusivity, transparency, accountability and access, the Supreme Court mandated the conducting of social audits in the implementation of the BOCW Act. It stated:[5]

> Our fourth direction is to the Ministry of Labour and Employment, the State Governments and the UTAs to

conduct a social audit on the implementation of the BOCW Act so that in future there is better and more effective and meaningful implementation of the BOCW Act. The sanctity of laws enacted by Parliament must be acknowledged— laws are enacted for being adhered to and not for being flouted. The rule of law must be respected and along with it the human rights and dignity of building and construction workers must also be respected and acknowledged, to avoid a complete breakdown of the BOCW Act compounded by serious violations of Part III of the Constitution guaranteeing fundamental rights.

The Supreme Court's acknowledgement of the positive role that audits and accountability therein can play in facilitating construction workers, who by the very nature of their work are vulnerable and unorganized, has been another important breakthrough for the concept and discipline of social accountability.

For each of the above—and any other practical extension of social accountability—to be credible and not continue as an extension of the existing power play, proactive efforts need to be made by those facilitating these mechanisms to reach out to the most marginalized sections within the community to participate. Independent facilitation should not be confused with neutrality. Such mechanisms need to be oriented in favour of the marginalized and should positively tilt towards them.

Challenges

Social accountability is not just an end but also a means to an end, which is protecting and nurturing social democracy. It confronts the same set of challenges that emerge when power is confronted. And thus, the means to overcome these challenges need to be wider in scope than mere technical solutions. Social accountability faces some characteristic contemporary challenges.

Centralization of information, and no space for dissent: We are today having to assert our right to accountability within a paradigm where there is a pervasive shrinking of the access to credible information. With the state having control over the content and timing of release of official statistics, the 'news' reported through media, and unrestrained resource of funds to build concocted narratives on social media, knowing the truth is acknowledgement as overwhelming a battle as acting on it is. The use of digital technology in governance has resulted in the handing over of control to codes. In many quarters, dissent and confronting decisions through questioning is seen as an affront to the state. In light of the neoliberal economic agenda being pursued by the state today, any critique of public service delivery is seen as an active opportunity to defend the decision of the state to reduce public provisioning.

Privatization of state services: Attempts made by citizens, individually and collectively, to expose corruption and unpack decisions with the objective of holding the state to account, reduce arbitrary decision-making and improve the functioning of public services are under threat of being co-opted by the state and corporate lobbies to justify privatization of public services instead. Where not outrightly privatized, multiple points in the service delivery chain where the state has 'outsourced' functions to the private sector adds to the complicated nexus of seeking accountability.

Weakening of independent accountability institutions: Through amendments, and the appointments of pliable individuals, there is a deliberate attempt to weaken independent democratic institutions such as the Election Commission, Information Commission, Human Rights Commission, and even the Supreme Court of India. As a result, persons holding the highest offices of power seem to violate the Constitution without being held accountable for it. In such a scenario of grand impunity, seeking accountability of the front-end functionary for denying basic services to those who are entitled to it seems like a petty issue, whereas for many people it is a battle for survival.

Eventually, it is all a continuum. The principles of social accountability are, as Ambedkar said, intrinsically related to liberty, equality and fraternity in a fundamental sense. Those who followed Ambedkar's call of 'Educate, organize, and struggle' have as a result of all three come up with extremely perceptive and useful applied principles such as the Bhilwara Principles. In the end, it is from practice and the struggles of marginalized people that wisdom, theory and peoples' legislation will emerge. Its implementation will depend on how well it deals with the inequalities of society, to make its contribution to a more just and equal society.

The Right to Education and Health: Is the State Giving Up?

Ambarish Rai, Srijita Majumder and Dipa Sinha

Education and health are central to achieving a dignified life for all. While the Constitution of India now explicitly recognizes the right to education, a number of Supreme Court judgments and the spirit of the Directive Principles of the Indian Constitution imply that the right to healthcare is also something that is accepted. Education and health have both intrinsic as well as instrumental worth as they are valuable on their own and also contribute to overall well-being through their influence on productivity and incomes. Although education and health remained neglected areas for a long time, the country seemed to have moved on to a positive trajectory in this regard in the 2000s with the introduction of the Sarva Shiksha Abhiyan (SSA) (in 2001) and the National Rural Health Mission (in 2005). The right to education became a fundamental right in 2001 by the eighty-sixth Constitutional Amendment, and the Right to Education (RTE) Act, enacted in 2009, made it a reality. This was a historic step towards the universalization of education in

India, made possible by the civil society movement, judicial intervention and international commitments.

While there have been significant improvements, health and education outcomes in India still remain poor and uneven, calling for continued and greater investments in these sectors with reforms to strengthen the government programmes in a manner such that they deliver. Instead of focusing on improving the delivery of public services, what has been observed over the last five years is a significant push towards privatization with fewer resources being allocated publicly. The crisis in public health became even more apparent in the wake of COVID-19, which exposed the huge gaps in health infrastructure and access to personal protective equipment (PPE), staff, test kits and so on.

Low Investment in Health and Education

In the last few years, we have witnessed an immense lack of political will that has resulted in the weakening of public education and health systems in India, making way for private players to enter and reap benefits. Despite education being a fundamental right, investment in education has declined substantially over the last few years, with only 3.5 per cent of GDP being allocated to education,[1] whereas back in 1966, the Kothari Commission had recommended spending 6 per cent of GDP on education (Kothari Commission Report, 1964). Health allocations have been historically low, with currently only about 1.4 per cent of GDP being allocated to health, while the National Policy on Health, 2017, makes a commitment of spending 2.5 per cent of GDP on health by 2025.[2] The Union government's spending on health as a percentage of the GDP reached an all-time low in 2015–16, even lower than in the much-tainted early 1990s.[3] Given such a low base, the Government of India announced only an additional Rs 15,000 crore (~0.1 per cent of GDP) in

March 2020 for COVID-19 emergency response and health system preparedness. Moreover, about half of this is supposed to be spent over the next four years![4]

Although there has been some revival in the last two years, it is nowhere near adequate and still doesn't match the peak attained earlier. The central government's spending on school education is mainly through the Samagra Shiksha Abhiyan (which integrated SSA, Rashtriya Madhyamik Shiksha Abhiyan [RMSA] and Teacher Education) which has a meagre allocation of Rs 36,322 crore in the Union Budget 2019–20. Another issue of concern with education is that cess has become the main source of funding for education, with 63.5 per cent[5] of the government's total expenditure in education coming from cess. Cess was supposed to contribute additionally to education over and above what the government routinely allocates.

There are more than nine lakh (9,00,316)[6] teacher vacancies at the elementary level, and only 53.8 per cent schools have three WASH facilities (drinking water, toilet and handwashing). Even after the RTE Act, 2009, more than 4.5 crore children remain out of school.[7] The scenario in health is not very different, with almost 25 per cent of the sanctioned doctors' positions in primary health centres (PHCs) remaining vacant, and only 7 per cent of health sub-centres functioning as per the Indian Public Health Standards (IPHS).[8]

Increasing Privatization

Recent policy developments in both education and health point towards a shift in strategy towards greater privatization and a reliance on the private sector through public-private partnerships (PPPs) towards the delivery of these services. The concerns with privatization are many, the central one being equity in access and exclusion of the poor and the marginalized.

One such example is the recently launched SATH-E (Sustainable Action for Transforming Human Capital in Education) project by the NITI Aayog in three states, Jharkhand, Madhya Pradesh and Odisha, with the Boston Consulting Group (BCG) and the Piramal Foundation for Education Leadership (PFEL) as knowledge partners. One of the major achievements of this project, as listed on the NITI Aayog website, is the school mergers and remediation programme. In Jharkhand, more than 6000 schools have been merged and this has proved to be a major hassle for primary-school children living in remote areas who find it difficult to travel. As a result, many children are compelled to remain at home.[9] Apart from the aforementioned three states, school closure has been witnessed in other parts of the country as well. According to data collected by the RTE Forum in six states (Madhya Pradesh, Jharkhand, Chhattisgarh, Uttarakhand, Odisha and Maharashtra), there have been more than 50,000 school closures/mergers.

At a time when 8.4 crore children (Census 2011) still remain outside the education system, the draft National Education Policy (NEP 2019) encourages both public and private sectors to construct different kinds of schools so that there is a healthy competition among them and parents can exercise choice. However, the vast majority of poor and marginalized parents cannot afford to exercise this choice. This choice is available only to the children of the elite class. The focus of the government should be on strengthening the public education system as millions of children cannot afford to go to fee-paying private schools. Instead of doing this, what we are witnessing today is the handing over of schools by the government to private entities, which enables them to reap profits.

In health too, the major initiative of the present government (in its first term and continuing in the present term) is on providing health insurance coverage to a targeted group of the population.

The Ayushman Bharat—Pradhan Mantri Jan Arogya Yojana (PMJAY) is basically an expansion of the Rashtriya Swasthya Bima Yojana (RSBY) and numerous other government-funded health insurance (GFHI) schemes run by state governments. The main provisions of PMJAY include hospital coverage of up to Rs 5 lakh for about ten crore families. It has now been rolled out in most states in the country (except Delhi, Odisha and West Bengal). Patients can avail of hospitalized care in either public or accredited private hospitals. The services are supposed to be provided cashless for the patients, while the hospitals are reimbursed based on package rates that are negotiated and updated regularly. There are a number of issues with this strategy, which one can foresee based on the experience of RSBY in India as well as similar insurance-based schemes in other countries.

While the main objective of this scheme is to reduce out-of-pocket expenditure on health (OoPE), its ability to do so is limited. Firstly, a large proportion of OoPE is on outpatient care (two-thirds) which is not even covered under this scheme. Secondly, with the skewed availability of hospitals, beneficiaries closer to urban centres and big cities tend to get some benefit while those in remote areas are left with no access.[10] In the absence of investments in the public sector because of the enhanced expenditure on such schemes, a large number of people are possibly excluded from accessing healthcare. Evidence based on the experience of RSBY shows that even with insurance, people end up spending out-of-pocket and that too much more in private hospitals compared to public hospitals.[11] Further, PMJAY is a targeted scheme covering about 40 per cent of the population, and previous experience with targeting in India (BPL) shows that there are huge inclusion and exclusion errors, often keeping out some of the most needy. Insurance-based strategies are also more expensive and the costs are expected to escalate. In just over a year of the implementation of PMJAY, there are already protests by the private sector that the package rates are too low, and there revisions have been made. On the other hand, since the pool of funds available for health is small, this leads to expenditure on primary healthcare services suffering.[12]

The problems of such an approach which expects the private sector to fill in for the gaps in the provision of public services is exacerbated with the poor regulatory mechanism in the country. Private schools and hospitals mushroom across the country, charging high fees, with no accountability over quality to the public or the government. Provisions such as 25 per cent of seats in private schools to be reserved for students from economically weaker sections (EWS) under the RTE Act or the rules mandating reservation of free beds for poor patients in private hospitals remain largely unimplemented in most parts of the country. Private institutions get away with huge tax benefits and other sops on the one hand, while they do not even fulfil their basic public responsibilities on the other. The private sector in health and education is of course varied, with a large not-for-profit sector which also makes positive contributions. But from the point of view of policy, relying on the private sector cannot be a substitute for the government providing universal public services.

National Policy

A national policy on health was introduced in 2017 and a draft NEP 2019 has been made public. We look at these two policies briefly.

National Education Policy[13]

There are some positive recommendations mentioned in the draft NEP 2019, such as the extension of the RTE Act to include children from the ages of three to six years and thirteen to eighteen years within its ambit; the removal of all para teachers; the non-involvement of teachers in non-academic duties; and a review of the second amendment to the RTE Act (which had withdrawn the no-detention policy) and a recommendation for school management committees in private schools. However, there are certain objectionable recommendations in the policy which deserve further analysis. The premise of the policy is that the quality of school education has been compromised in India due to the priorities of equity and access. Such an analysis is deeply problematic. Firstly, the Indian school education system is one of the most inequitable in the world. Secondly, the understanding of quality to mean only learning scores is a very narrow approach to education. Equity is also an important objective of providing school education and therefore it is a part of good-quality education.

The policy further recommends dilution of norms to make them 'less restrictive'. RTE norms set the benchmark of quality, and it is a legal right. Not specifying a common minimum standard below which schools cannot fall creates conditions where the quality of facilities in some schools only sinks lower and further perpetuates inequality.

Another objectionable suggestion is that different agents—both public and private—should be enabled to construct different kinds of schools so that there is healthy competition among them and the parents can exercise choice. This ignores the reality in India where the vast majority of poor and marginalized parents simply cannot avail of this choice. Universalization of school education cannot be a reality in India without an equitable system delivering quality education. India's multi-tiered education system is one of the biggest challenges in school education, and the draft document, by encouraging the private philanthropic sector, will lead to the further entrenchment of private players in education.

Even after the RTE Act is extended to pre-primary and secondary education, as suggested in the committee's report, and the revised Act implemented within a new time frame, school education in India is likely to remain a den of discrimination and a source of perpetuating and accelerating economic and social inequality. This is principally because the continuance, even under the revised RTE regime, of the existing multilayered school education system is inherently discriminatory. The only way to remove this built-in discrimination is to introduce a Common School System (CSS) which ensures a uniform quality of education to all children. The CSS was first recommended by the Kothari Commission (1964–66) and reaffirmed in the National Education Policies in 1968 and 1986, as amended in 1992. However, there is no mention of a CSS in the draft NEP.

While the policy recommends the recruitment of 'highly qualified and professionally trained' teachers, the NEP has recommended the deployment of student teachers and educated members of the community as teachers and volunteer teachers. There are issues with the two main recommendations of the NEP for removing learning deficiency of children in schools, viz. the NTP (National Tutors Programme) and RIAP (Remedial Instructional Aides Programme). These suggestions go against the RTE Act, which has no provision for special tutoring for students who are deficient in learning, rather the provision of special training, which is open to all those who want to attend it. This training is supposed to be given in the school and run by teachers; not by fellow students, community members or other volunteers, as suggested by the NEP.

National Health Policy

One of the initiatives of the Modi government has been to put forward the National Health Policy (NHP), 2017. Drafted in an environment of growing motivation for social health insurance schemes on the way towards universal health coverage (UHC), the NHP focuses on universal access to comprehensive services through increased investment, institutional reforms, and the remodelling and expansion of primary healthcare which is comprehensive and free for every citizen. For secondary care, the NHP proposes to use strategic purchasing as a means to expand services. The policy also talks about focusing on preventive, curative and palliative care to be provided through the 'public sector with a focus on quality'. The policy further places an emphasis on stopping the growth of non-communicable diseases and the need for addressing the social determinants of health, the integration of AYUSH and national programmes, increasing the financial investment for health, the exemption of user fees and dispensing of free drugs and consumables, and developing a referral system for steady patient flow.

The NHP has an explicit focus on promoting private investment in health and engaging the private sector for various aspects of service delivery, mainly for secondary and tertiary care through strategic purchasing; for primary care in urban areas; for training and skill development; disaster management, etc. While the NHP talks about many things, there is not much movement in terms of increased funds or programmes on anything but this aspect of the policy. As seen above, the PMJAY has set in motion the process of promoting private investment in health and engaging the private sector more. On the other hand, there is no progress on the objective of increasing public healthcare spending to 2.5–3 per cent of the GDP as stated in the policy, with public spending on health as a proportion of the GDP not increasing throughout this government's rule. The NDA regime has in fact cut public spending on health, as seen above, which clearly contradicts its own objectives of augmenting public investment. Critics in fact suggest that the NHP favours a limited set of basic services to be provided by public facilities, with people being left at the mercy of the private sector for most services.

In the current context, with the changes in fiscal architecture brought about by the Fourteenth Finance Commission, whereby state governments have been devolved more untied funds, whereas sector-specific funds are being squeezed, one likely impact could be on social sector spending, particularly in states with an unfavourable fiscal situation or a lower priority towards the social sector. In order to enhance public spending significantly, as aspired in various policy documents including the High Level Expert Group (HLEG) report of the erstwhile Planning Commission, various plan documents and the latest NHP 2017, it is imperative that a coordinated effort from both the Centre and the states be made to increase spending, particularly in areas of primary care and preventive health services. Under the current regime, marred by cutbacks in spending on health, such possibilities hardly exist.

Conclusion

In this brief overview of the education and health sectors, we have seen that providing education and healthcare for all in India continues to remain an elusive goal, with recent policy initiatives taking us in the opposite direction. While in the previous ten years, corresponding with UPA I and II, there were some efforts made to bring public education and healthcare provision centre-stage through the RTE and National Health Mission, the approach now is more on quick-fix solutions involving the private sector and largely ignoring equity considerations. Poor investments in both sectors continue to be the trend. Huge human resource gaps exist in education as well as health which need to be addressed immediately, both in light of improving service delivery and also in the context of the current employment crisis in the country. Regressive policies such as the withdrawal of the no–detention policy, the dilution of RTE norms, and diverting public resources to health insurance–based schemes while there is no strengthening of public systems need to be reconsidered. Strong regulatory mechanisms need to be put in place to ensure that the provision of health and education is not commodified to an extent where many are left out from their basic rights while others make unrestricted profits.

Education and health are basic rights and they have to be seen as such by both states as well as the general public. The state must therefore be held accountable for not providing these services to all. Doing so would require increasing budgetary allocations, investing in human resources and empowering local communities to hold the system accountable. The response to the COVID-19 crisis unfortunately shows that there is very little determination towards addressing these structural problems. This is one of the biggest challenges that the health sector in India has faced in recent times, and it could have been seen as an opportunity to begin strengthening the entire health system towards more equitable access to healthcare.

Despite the fact that the number of deaths due to other diseases such as tuberculosis are very high in India, the interventions that are in place to address these were literally put to a halt as the health system geared up to respond to the COVID-19 pandemic. The inequity in response when a disease also affects the rich and the middle class is glaring. A national lockdown may be justified to slow the spread of the infection, and to give the country time to prepare its health sector. But as mentioned above, sufficient resources have not been allocated for this.

Issues such as a large number of vacancies and the crumbling primary healthcare infrastructure afflict the health system in many parts of the country, and the efforts at containing and dealing with this outbreak will have been on the foundations of this very weak edifice. The Rural Health Statistics of the MoHFW, for instance, shows that 24.9 per cent of doctors' positions in sub-centres and PHCs remain vacant. There are also a large number of vacancies in the posts of health assistants, male health workers, lab technicians and pharmacists. The shortfall and vacancies of specialists at community health centres (CHCs) are even higher, with 73.7 per cent of positions lying vacant. There are also massive gaps in availability of functional buildings, drinking water, toilet facilities, etc., in health centres. Community health workers such as ASHAs (accredited social health activists) and ANMs (auxiliary nurse midwives) are already overburdened by the number of tasks assigned to them under poor working conditions. In these circumstances, while acknowledging that the government has made some positive efforts in terms of ordering more ventilators and PPE, it is also the case that this is not enough. Far more resources have to be poured into the health system so that the public provision of healthcare is strengthened. At the same time, the private sector, which currently provides most of the healthcare in the country, needs to be made to play its role by ensuring the pooling of resources, greater regulation and more accountability. It is regrettable that the same enthusiasm with which a lockdown has been implemented is not being shown for building a more resilient healthcare system.

MGNREGA: A Distress Saviour or a Saviour in Distress?

Rajendran Narayanan and Annie Raja[1]

Several progressive rights-based legislations such as the Right to Information, the Forest Rights Act, the National Food Security Act—to name a few—were enacted during the UPA regime between 2004 and 2013. Frequent droughts, lack of work and low wages in rural areas have meant that the most marginalized rural poor have been subject to distress migration to towns and cities. Such migration increases their defencelessness, making women and children in particular more vulnerable to exploitation and bearing the brunt of severe indignity. The enactment of the landmark Mahatma Gandhi National Rural Employment Guarantee Act, 2005, is a way to address some of these challenges. It is, in principle, a significant departure from earlier public works programmes because it provides a legislative framework for the right to work, fructifying the constitutional right to life. Since its enactment, it has been a subject of much public discussion. Its merits and demerits have been scrutinized and debated on the civilian, political and academic arenas alike. Indeed, referring to this programme, Prime Minister Narendra

Modi had said in 2015,[2] 'MGNREGA is a living monument of your failures. After sixty years of Independence, you had to send people to dig holes. This is a monument of your failures, and I am going to carry on beating the drum about it with much fanfare. I will tell the world that the pits you are digging, they are the result of your sins for sixty years.' While it would be an overstatement to say that MGNREGA is a panacea to cure poverty, the above statement is, however, in poor taste and merits condemnation. In fact, in the light of the continued unemployment and agrarian crisis, which we have highlighted below, a well implemented MGNREGA can be a huge relief for the poor.

The recently released Periodic Labour Force Survey (PLFS)[3] Report for 2017–18 presents a grim picture about India's employment situation. As per the report, India is going through an unprecedented unemployment crisis with an unemployment rate of 6.1 per cent—the worst since 1972. Since 2011–12, as per the usual status, the unemployment rate has increased by three times among rural men and doubled among rural women. Let us look at some more broad statistics to get a perspective. According to the Socio-economic and Caste Census (SECC)[4] of 2011, more than 56 per cent of households do not own land, and more than 51 per cent depend on casual manual labour as the main source of income. More than 62 per cent of land does not have assured irrigation for growing two crops a year, and less than 10 per cent of rural households own any irrigation equipment. According to the Drought Early Warning System,[5] a real-time drought monitoring system, as on 2 August 2019, around 42 per cent of the country was facing abnormally dry to exceptionally dry conditions, and 16 per cent was facing severe to exceptionally dry conditions. This ecological situation is alarming as well as perplexing given that parts of Karnataka and Kerala were submerged in floods in 2019.

The rural poor are the most vulnerable in the face of such lack of employment and the alternating pattern of droughts and floods. These are recipes for distress migration from rural to urban areas. While rural India is in misery, the economic conditions in urban India have reportedly been as bad. As per news reports,[6] the urban unemployment rate for all ages crossed 9 per cent between January and March 2019. As per PLFS data, the labour force participation rate (LFPR) for all ages, measuring the proportion of the working-age population that is either employed or seeking employment, has decreased from 39.5 per cent in 2012 to 36.9 per cent in 2018. What this means is that despite the decrease in the proportion of people employed or seeking work, there is an increase in the unemployment levels. This is extremely worrying. Even among regular urban workers, as Ishan Anand and Anjana Thampi[7] show, 45 per cent earn less than Rs 10,000 a month, and one-third of women earn less than Rs 5000 a month. There are at least three major concerns here. First, lack of work opportunities in rural areas would increase migration to urban areas, thereby exacerbating the urban unemployment situation. Second, an increase in urban labour force would decrease the already low urban daily labour wages even more. Third, the living conditions of footloose migrant workers in urban areas are deplorable and an increased migration would worsen it.

What we are therefore facing is a grave two-pronged crisis: socio-economic catastrophe on the one hand and severe agrarian and ecological distress on the other. It is in these socio-economic and environmental contexts that one needs to further underscore the importance of the MGNREGA. The MGNREGA's provisions amount to justiciable rights—the right to work on demand, the right to unemployment allowance if work is not provided within fifteen days, the right to payment of wages within fifteen days, the right to minimum wages, essential worksite facilities, among others. In addition to the worker-centric rights to empower the vulnerable populace, the Act envisages relief from ecological and agrarian distress by the creation of long-term sustainable assets through water and soil conservation, drought proofing, renovation of water bodies, rural connectivity, etc.

The Act, therefore, promises several recognizable benefits. Most notably, there was much hope that the Act would reduce poverty and enable a redistribution of power between the state and the rural poor in favour of the latter. While there is no reason to believe that employment for 100 days in a year at minimum wages will eradicate poverty altogether, this programme can provide significant relief in times of peak distress. Also, the radical redistribution of power through the strengthening of local governance has not exactly panned out. Corruption still persists, albeit the forms and methods are different and aided by the technology architecture of the MGNREGA in many places. We look at some of the positives and potentials of the MGNREGA to alleviate the twin crises outlined earlier. We also present a view and cite instances of how the implementation of the Act has been subverted in letter and spirit, largely due to the lack of political will and through an over-reliance on techno-utopianism.

In spite of the programme functioning at half its mandated capacity (the average number of days worked per household has been around forty-seven days[8] for the last five years) and despite numerous implementation challenges, it has had a far-reaching impact. Five broad positive aspects can be identified: (a) it is universal and not targeted; (b) increase in rural incomes; (c) countering of gender and caste inequalities; (d) quality asset creation; and (e) community empowerment.

The Act is universal across rural India and not targeted. What this means is that the most vulnerable will self-select to work in this programme. There is substantial evidence to demonstrate that universal schemes are less prone to corruption than targeted schemes. In targeted programmes, it is very common to have errors of inclusion and exclusion. Inclusion errors arise when undeserving people get recorded as beneficiaries and get entitlements that are not due to them. Exclusion errors happen when genuine beneficiaries get left out. Such errors go unrecorded and people continue to be left out. Exclusion errors have more severe consequences as the individuals excluded fall through the cracks of policymaking and democracy at large.

The universal nature of the MGNREGA has meant that it has served as a lifeline for the poorest with one out of every three rural households having worked in the programme. According to the official MGNREGA website,[9] in 2018–19, close to eighty million (eight crore) people[10] worked under the MGNREGA. According to the 2011 Government of India census, SC/ST households form about 30 per cent of the rural population and largely constitute the poorest sections in the society. Around 40 per cent of the total households employed under the MGNREGA every year belong to SC and ST households. Data from the Employment–Unemployment Survey of the National Sample Survey (NSS) shows an eightfold increase in participation in public works in 2009–10 over 2004–05, confirming the impact of the MGNREGA. The India Human Development Survey (IHDS), a joint effort of the National Council of Applied Economic Research (NCAER) and the University of Maryland, surveyed 27,000 rural households before the Act (2004–05) and after the Act was implemented in all districts (2011–12). This is a nationally representative survey and a rich source of data presenting an opportunity to assess the reach and impact of the MGNREGA.

Indeed, based on this survey, Sonalde Desai, Prem Vashishtha and Omkar Joshi[11] point out that the self-targeting nature of the MGNREGA plays out well, less than expected but significant nevertheless. Work uptake in villages with poorer infrastructure is higher compared to the better-off ones. Dalits (36 per cent) and Adivasis (30 per cent) are much more likely to participate in the programme than other households (20 per cent). Only 10 per cent of the top consumption quintile participate, meaning that people in the higher wealth bracket choose to not work in the MGNREGA despite having the option to. Desai, Vashishtha and Joshi show that about 30 per cent of households with no literate adult participate compared to only 13 per cent of households with a single literate adult. Children pay a heavy price in the poverty trap. They also show that due to the MGNREGA, school enrolment increased, so child labour potentially decreased, and MGNREGA incomes were used to buy books. These are significant results indicating that the programme acts as a huge economic safety net for those who are most in need.

There has been much questioning about the role of the MGNREGA in increasing rural incomes. Based on a large-scale randomized experiment in Andhra Pradesh, Karthik Muralidharan, Paul Niehaus and Sandip Sukhtankar[12] show that the incomes of MGNREGA workers increased by 13 per cent and overall poverty fell by 17 per cent between 2010 and 2012. Moreover, 90 per cent of the income gains, according to their study, are due to an increase in market earnings through a spillover effect of a well-functioning MGNREGA. Stefan Klonner and Christian Oldiges[13] showed that the Act has increased consumption among SC/ST households during the agricultural lean season by as much as 30 per cent and reduced poverty by about 50 per cent between 2006 and 2008. Using a different methodology, Desai, Vashishtha and Joshi demonstrate that 32 per cent of poverty reduction for MGNREGA participants was due to MGNREGA employment. Fourteen million persons would have become poor without the MGNREGA.[14] Himanshu and Sujata Kundu[15] (and several references therein) demonstrate that after stagnating for at least three decades, the growth in real rural wages (especially agriculture) picked up in 2007–08 following the inception of the MGNREGA. Lack of access to money in times of dire need has been a key source of exploitation of the vulnerable by local elites and moneylenders. The poorest have no option but to resort to borrowing money from such lenders. In many parts of the country, the interest rates for such borrowing can be as punishing as 100 per cent per year. According to the IHDS survey, the reliance on moneylenders decreased by 21 per cent from 2004–05 to 2011–12 for households working in the MGNREGA. Electronic fund transfers in the MGNREGA started as far back as 2011 through the Electronic Fund Management System (eFMS). This became central to the project of financial inclusion. Since eFMS started in 2011, labour wages started getting directly transferred to the workers' banks/postal accounts. This, in turn, had a positive impact as far as independence from local moneylenders was concerned. Access to formal borrowing structures through banks paralleled the decline in exploitative borrowing from local elites. The MGNREGA's early stated emphasis on creating bank accounts can take credit for this.

The role of women in the MGNREGA needs special attention. Being the first programme to ensure wage parity for both men and women, the Act has played a significant role in improving women's participation in the labour force. According to the IHDS survey cited before, nearly 45 per cent female MGNREGA workers were either not working or working only on a family farm in 2004–05. The MGNREGA was thus the first opportunity for such women to be brought into the paid workforce. In fact, in the last five years, more than half of all MGNREGA works were done by women.

Mehtabul Azam[16] shows that the daily wages for casual work for women increased by 8 per cent due to the MGNREGA. This has been consistently evident from the early days of the programme. The following early testimony of Bhagwati Ram from Khaira panchayat of Rajnandgaon district, Chhattisgarh, illustrates this: 'Before MGNREGA, we were forced to work as agricultural labourers or casual labourers in brick kilns for Rs 25 to 30 per day. But under MGNREGA we are getting Rs 62 to 64 per day, which is almost an unexpected amount for us.' While the recorded increase in daily wages for women is still low, it is nevertheless compelling given how low the baseline wages prior to the Act were. Though women were doing all farm and non-farm activities and their labour has always been an integral part of the rural household, it remained invisible as they never earned any money for it.

Moreover, as per the IHDS survey, the ability to seek healthcare among women MGNREGA workers showed a 14 per cent increase compared to those who didn't work under the MGNREGA. Broad statistics aside, the programme has accorded a fillip to the dignity of women. Many women were economically dependent on their husbands. While this may still be true to some extent, with the availability of MGNREGA work within the panchayat, women now exercise autonomy in choosing when and where to work. As Sumathi from Maruwai panchayat of Cuddalore district, Tamil Nadu, said: 'I used to depend on my husband for any expense but now I am earning and also contributing to the household expenditure.'[17] Further, since women's labour wages are directly deposited into their bank accounts, their capacity to save and participate in self-help groups has increased.[18] Numerous other intangible positives, which we take for granted, such as the ability of a mother to send her child to the local 'English-medium school', to be able to buy a birthday gift for the child, buy more vegetables or be able to go to the village fair, remain unmetrizable. Such progressive gender-balancing legislation is indeed a landmark initiative in a country where the mental, physical and social oppression of women continues to be deplorable.

However, in line with Prime Minister Modi's comment, there are several critics of the MGNREGA, such as Jagdish Bhagwati and Arvind Panagariya.[19] While some assets created through the MGNREGA may indeed be unproductive, claims such as 'wasteful projects' are, however, one-sided and reductive. Evidence on MGNREGA assets suggests a different narrative from the 'dole-hole' view of the sceptics. To begin with, it is no mean feat that over the years more than twenty million different assets under the MGNREGA have been completed. The scale of implementation of such a programme was unprecedented. Therefore, an important chunk of the first few years was spent establishing the political, administrative and technical architecture for such a large programme. Moreover, to truly assess the productivity of assets and their multiplier effects in the economy, one needs to observe their use for a long time. For instance, say the cost of creating a well is Rs 50,000. It might take three years just to recover the cost. Its true benefit can be understood when one evaluates how it has benefited farmers and improved productivity over a ten- to fifteen-year time horizon. In addition, prior to the creation of such an asset, people would have had to travel long distances to fetch water but now it is easily available. Therefore, profits obtained from these assets need to be calculated over the lifetime of the assets. Nevertheless, numerous studies related to asset quality created through the MGNREGA suggest that it has had a positive, transformational role in agriculture, and water and soil conservation. Sudha Narayanan[20] presents an impressive compendium of academic findings outlining the positive impacts of assets. In particular, she classifies the findings pertaining to the impact of assets into four meaningful dimensions: (a) augmenting rural incomes; (b) augmenting agricultural productivity through investments in land and water; (c) building environmental resilience through plantation; and (d) mitigating natural disasters. Consider the following handful of examples from extensive academic literature to illustrate the positive impact: In a drought-prone area such as Cuddapah district of Andhra Pradesh, the construction of trenches through the MGNREGA has increased water availability for irrigation, which has increased farm incomes. By studying more than 140 best performing water conservation assets in seventy-five villages across four states, Shilp Verma and Tushaar Shah[21] show that each of them recovered the investment within just one year of use.

To address repeated drought, the government of Jharkhand sanctioned wells to increase access to irrigation. Anjor Bhaskar and Pankaj Yadav[22] show that such wells yield a rate of return of 6 per cent. Assets studied by Rakesh Tiwari et al.[23] and Tashina Esteves et al.[24] show that they have reduced the vulnerability of agricultural production, water resources and livelihoods to uncertain rainfall, water scarcity and poor soil fertility. In a survey of more than 4100 assets and over 4800 users across Maharashtra, Sudha Narayanan et al.[25] show that farmers viewed water conservation and harvesting works through the MGNREGA as enablers of crop production and as expanding the area under cultivation. Further, they show that each rupee spent on horticulture yields Rs 3 within just three years. From the lens of socio-economic gains, infrastructure work such as the creation of roads, panchayat bhavans, cremation structures, etc. have gained traction among people and have been found to be useful. However, they are not natural resource (NR)-based. Several other NR-based assets such as farm bunds, wells and tree plantation works are critical for the restoration of rural ecology. By studying a mix of NR (farm bunding, tree plantation works, wells) assets and non-NR (roads, toilets) assets in two sample districts of Madhya Pradesh, Anjor Bhaskar, Amod Shah[26] and Sunil Gupta[26] estimate the 'greenness' of MGNREGA works. By creating a 'green index', they find that the MGNREGA is fulfilling its potential of creating green jobs. For example, three years after the construction of a farm bund in Harbhajan Dhurve's farm in Chhindwara, there has been a two-fold increase in agricultural output leading to savings of 155 kilolitres of groundwater annually and a 33 per cent reduction in water extraction. This, in turn, meant that there was less use of pumps to extract water, thus significantly reducing diesel consumption and leading to an overall reduction of 416 kg of carbon-dioxide emissions. There is much variation in asset quality across the country, and these examples may not be nationally representative. However, what these examples demonstrate is the immense potential of the positive impact of the assets, from a socio-economic perspective as well as a means to mitigate drought-effects, improve agricultural productivity, restore the ecology, and promote soil and water conservation.

There are several other aspects of the MGNREGA that are much less flattering and need urgent attention. Much of these are to do with a lack of political and administrative will. Most notably, the MGNREGA is a demand-driven programme in the sense that work should be given to a job card holder within fifteen days of applying for work. However, the programme has become supply-driven because of the constraints imposed on financial allocations. Since 2014, many civil society groups have consistently pointed out the pernicious manner in which funds have been squeezed and the damaging domino effect it has had on the programme overall. First, contrary to the repeated claims of the finance minister every year since 2014, adjusting for inflation, the budget in each of the last five years has been lower than the allocations made as early as

2010–11. Second, about one-sixth of the budget allocation in each of the last five years is of pending wage liabilities from previous years. It was the worst in 2016–17 when pending liabilities were 35 per cent (Rs 13,220 crore) out of a total allocation of Rs 38,500 crore. This has led to a vicious cycle with crores of workers left in the lurch without wages for work done by them. Third, World Bank economists Rinku Murgai and Martin Ravallion[27] recommended that at least 1.7 per cent of the GDP must be allocated for the programme to run robustly. But the allocations for the MGNREGA as a percentage of GDP in each of the last five years have been consistently low, just around 0.30 per cent, despite an increase in the tax to GDP ratio.[28] Fourth, the lack of funds, among other critical factors, has resulted in inordinate delays in the payment of wages.

Wage payments to MGNREGA workers happen in two stages. The first stage corresponds to the time taken by the blocks to generate the electronic Funds Transfer Orders (FTOs) and send them digitally to the central government. The second stage is the time taken by the central government to process these FTOs and transfer wages to workers' accounts. While it is true that delays in the first stage have reduced, those in the second stage continue to be unacceptably high. By analysing over 90 lakh transactions, Rajendran Narayanan, Sakina Dhorajiwala and Rajesh Golani[29] found that only about 21 per cent of the payments are credited on time; the central government takes more than fifty days (which is the second stage) to transfer wages to workers. It has wilfully suppressed information pertaining to delays caused by it in wage transfer, leading to a gross under-calculation of the workers' legal right to delay compensation. In a memorandum dated 21 August 2017, the Ministry of Finance acknowledged that the delay in payments was directly linked to the lack of 'availability of funds'. This glaring lacuna was argued in the Supreme Court in a public interest litigation (*Swaraj Abhiyan v. Union of India and Others*) where the Court gave a strong judgment[30] regarding payment delays.[31]

Fifth, the MGNREGA wage rates are less than the corresponding minimum wage for agriculture in thirty-three states and Union Territories.[32] While the minimum wage, as per the Seventh Pay Commission, is Rs 692 per day, the average MGNREGA wage rate in 2019–20 is Rs 179 per day. The Supreme Court has repeatedly upheld minimum wage as a fundamental right and has equated the payment of anything less as 'forced labour'.[33] Sixth, Rajendran Narayanan and Madhubala Pothula[34] demonstrate other methods by which the central government has been rationing funds for the programme. Unremunerative MGNREGA wages, coupled with the long delays in wage payments and even non-payment of wages in many cases, have turned many rural workers away from the employment guarantee programme.

Sixth, in lieu of strengthening the true potential of the MGNREGA, a combination of a lack of political will and techno-utopianism has reduced this programme to a technological laboratory. The chapter on the MGNREGA in the 2019 Economic Survey showcases the central government's invested energies on technology and markets as opposed to focusing on core, unaddressed issues such as funds allocation, timely wage payment, minimum wages and other rights. Indeed, technology needs to be harnessed and the complexity of the programme dictates the digitization of transactions based on strong principles of transparency and accountability. Mandatory proactive disclosure of information in the MGNREGA, through multiple modes, online and offline, is a legal mandate. While this mandate has begun to be institutionalized through its real-time, transaction-based Management Information System (MIS) to some extent, however, the disclosure of information to workers (the primary stakeholders) in an accessible manner continues to be disregarded. The MGNREGA is one of the few programmes that can be subject to public scrutiny given the sheer amount of information related to its implementation and status that is supposed to be in the public domain.

However, the authors' experience of working with MGNREGA labourers has shown that the MIS is being routinely tampered with by the central government without any record of decisions and public accountability. Consider the following few examples: (a) The law requires the government to pay unemployment allowance to those who demand work and fail to get it in fifteen days. Despite the evident difference between work demanded and employment provided, the unemployment allowance is rarely ever paid. (b) Projected labour budgets of previous years submitted by states have been manipulated to match the amount of funds available. (c) Concealed restrictions on programme implementation, such as preventing demand registration or generation of attendance records if the district has exceeded its arbitrary cap of funds, are imposed through the MIS. (d) The MIS is being blatantly used to absolve the central government from its legal obligation of timely wage payments and full payment of compensation to workers in the event of delayed payments. The MIS, which can be a tool for both transparency and efficiency in digital governance, is instead being used to centralize control and conceal the liabilities of the government. Moreover, such centralization has also led to several cases of diverted payments (one person's payments going to somebody else's accounts), rejected payments and locked payments, to name a few. In this context, Ankita Aggarwal,[35] Sakina Dhorajiwala,[36] Jean Drèze[37] and Debmalya Nandy[38] give numerous examples of the manner in which workers' rights have been compromised.

This brings us to the final point about local governance. The planning of works for the MGNREGA was envisioned to happen through the participation of resident communities at the gram sabhas (village councils). The idea was to strengthen institutions of local governance, in line with the Seventy-third Amendment of the Constitution. This was meant to give a platform and an opportunity for the poorer and more vulnerable communities to have a better say in local implementation. This has, however, largely remained elusive. Barring some cases, the implementation has largely been top-down. The higher-level bureaucrats tend to control the programme (such as dictating the type of works to be done) and impose constraints on the field-level bureaucrats (such as limiting the registration of demand for work due to lack of funds). These have adverse consequences. For a variety of reasons—perhaps political—there has been a push to create individual assets such as construction of houses using the MGNREGA. Individuals can utilize ninety-five days of MGNREGA wages as labour cost for this. There is no denying that such individual assets are critical. But such individual infrastructure projects may not be the priority for a local community which does not have a stake in the decision-making process. Such projects are usually target-driven. On many occasions, the bureaucracy has to meet targets of completing a designated number of private infrastructure works, again perhaps for political gains. This is antithetical to the core aims of the demand-driven, decentralized decision-making aspects of the MGNREGA.

In conclusion, the Act has tremendous power and potential to transform rural livelihoods and mitigate agrarian distress. As demonstrated, even when working in half its capacity, it has had many meaningful impacts. Other programmes and governance structures have much to learn and leverage from the MGNREGA—especially the principles of equity and justice as enshrined in the Act. But the prime minister's remark, doused in hubris, aptly demonstrates the government's intent to let this programme hang on tenterhooks. Shifting attention from the core issues—adequate fund allocation, timely payment of wages and higher wage rates—to tinkering with technological fixes has discouraged worker participation. With simmering unemployment and an agrarian crisis, it behoves the government to strengthen the core aspects of the programme, resuscitate it and give a new lease of life to the vulnerable. Adopting human-centred design principles for technology can greatly alleviate workers' woes and simultaneously streamline and ease work for the bureaucracy.

For example, the creation of Jan Soochna portals in Rajasthan where information is available in various panchayats, in formats for information dissemination designed collectively by workers, activists and government officials, seems like a promising human-centred proposition. Further, automatic calculation of unemployment allowance is great but it does not serve the purpose if it is not paid. One has to be mindful that accountability isn't sacrificed at the altar of technology. It is time that we pause, refocus our attention on how to strengthen worker participation and not let the technology obsession of the government stampede justiciable rights.

Finally, we should keep in mind the following valuable lines from Kentaro Toyama's book *Geek Heresy: Rescuing Social Change from the Cult of Technology*:[39]

> It's not that technocratic ideas in general are bad in and of themselves. Rather, the trouble is cultism and imbalance. New vaccines are good, but not while health-care systems go unfunded. Educational technology might be helpful, but not if good teachers and institutional support are lacking.

Elections are great, but not if social norms and government institutions don't support democracy. Technocratic means might be a part of the solution, but with so much attention on them, who's working on the other parts?

Key to Reducing Inequalities through Accountability, Transparency and Participation

N. Paul Divakar, Beena Pallical, Juno Varghese and Adikanda Singh

When India got its independence, millions of people celebrated with deep pride and gratitude. However, seventy-one years later, the country's oppressed castes, classes and religious minorities continue to be at the margins, with their equality and freedom being contested by the makers of laws themselves. Decades ago, the nationalist movement eventually secured political independence, freedom and equality for its citizens; however, Ambedkar's question of 'social freedom and justice' challenges us even today. Social justice is the apparition that the Indian Constitution strives to achieve. The Constitution directs the state to ensure and secure social justice and order on the basis of equal opportunity so that it is not denied to any citizen on any ground.

However, the lack of social justice and freedom is clearly evident during the current crisis in the country. Around the time this piece was sent to press, COVID-19 was declared a pandemic. While several countries are trying to make sense of the situation, India has taken some stringent measures to curb the virus and a full lockdown is in force. Millions of people have been dislodged, the public health gap is glaringly palpable, and the state has sprung into policing mode rather than being facilitative and enabling. Most marginalized communities have been pushed further into the margins, the traditional intergenerational systems like the caste system and untouchability have become accentuated even further. Unemployment has grown exponentially and the economy is on a dangerous downward spiral.

Apart from the overall implications for the economy and the people of the country, COVID-19 will have a catastrophic effect on the weakest communities. In India, the foremost strategy enforced by the government to contain the outbreak is that of 'social distancing'—or rather physical distancing—self-quarantine, personal hygiene and lockdown, without putting in place the required mechanisms to actually address this health crisis. Oppressive societal structures based on caste, class and patriarchy leave very little room for the already vulnerable to overcome the distress caused by the pandemic. The nature of COVID-19 has increased the vulnerability of Dalits and Adivasis and has impacted them disproportionately, especially women and children. The measures taken by the government have worsened the social seclusion and isolation they have faced for centuries. The unplanned lockdown has further exasperated the situation and can turn into an economic disaster for these sections, killing more people than the virus itself.

Even in these times, discrimination based on caste and gender is slowly coming to the fore. In Andhra Pradesh, Dalits are being prevented from using main roads and streets in the name of containing the community transmission of the pandemic. Around 1200 Dalits in Atmakur Mandal, Kurnool district, are required to travel through the main road of the SC (Scheduled Caste) Colony to KJ Road. However, leaders from the dominant caste have prevented them from doing so and have even threatened to burn down the entire colony if anyone is to trespass. They even call Dalits by their caste name in an attempt to humiliate and demean them.[1]

In another incident in Saharanpur, Uttar Pradesh, forty-four-year-old Dalit domestic worker Mamta was beaten up for protesting the denial of ration that was supposed to be distributed among the residents of Abhishek Nagar.[2] Meanwhile, a Dalit family in Haryana was attacked for not following the prime minister's call to turn off lights at 9 p.m. on 5 April 2020 to exercise a show of unity during this crisis.

Cleaners, *safai karamcharis*, sanitation workers and waste-pickers are narrating stories that are extremely disturbing. It is usually Dalits and Adivasis who are engaged in these occupations which are considered to be 'essential' services by the government. They are exposed to greater risk of the disease, but many of them are doing their jobs without any kind of PPE.

Furthermore, even though the finance ministry has announced special insurance cover for them, they will require an employment ID to authenticate their status as sanitation workers before they can claim this insurance. A recent report by CNN has put forth the issue of employment cards for informal workers. 'According to the Dalit Bahujan Resource Centre, 22% of sanitation workers, manual scavengers and waste-pickers did not have the 12-digit, biometric national identification number and 33% did not possess ration cards to get subsidized food through the public distribution system.'[3] Such treatment throws them deeper into poverty.

Wealth disparity is on the rise in the country, with the few at the top being the ones who own economic resources.

In fact, India remains one of the most unequal countries in the world, where development has transpired only among a few sections of the society.[4] Economic poverty is highest among the marginalized groups: women, Dalits, Adivasis and religious minorities, among others. 'There are a concatenation of forces and crisis in social, economic, political and cultural life combined by populists to reject the liberal order, social justice and traditional elites,' writes Kamal Mitra Chenoy. Neoliberalism, he adds, is one of the major factors leading to the rise of right-wing authoritarianism.[5] When we examine the country on the basis of five basic indicators—poverty, inequality, employment, violence and atrocities—the numbers are indicative of the marginalization of communities such as Dalits and Adivasis, leading to widening inequalities and growing disaffection. 'Entitlements to economic rights become narrower and narrower the farther down the hierarchical ladders of the caste system. Without intervention, classically untouchables, or Dalits, who lie at the very bottom of the social order, find themselves restricted to the most despised occupations and the lowest wages,' write Katherine S. Newman and Sukhadeo Thorat.[6] They further add that Dalits find themselves repressed as citizens and are often restricted and denied in practice civil rights (freedom of expression, equality before the law), political rights (the ability to exercise political power) and socio-economic rights (claims to property, employment and education).

In the recent past, one has seen an absolute misuse of power in amending people's progressive legislations to undermine the power of the people and give more powers to the state. One example of this is the Right to Information (RTI) Act, which is mostly used by marginalized communities to strengthen governance processes, but amendments which are detrimental to the effective functioning of this Act have been passed recently.[7]

This threat of regressive development lies like a dark shroud, mostly affecting weaker sections of society.

There is growing inequality, joblessness and a socio-economic crisis, combined with rising intolerance and hate crimes, rejecting the 'secular' and 'socialist' orientation of the Constitution. Marginalized sections are being deprived of their rights vigorously. The country is witnessing a rise in violence in the name of a Hindu nationalist agenda, creating a condition of 'normalization' of violence.[8]

Caste-based Inequalities and Exclusion

Caste-based discrimination continues to be one of the widest-ranging human rights violations that has been prevailing for decades, causing affected communities to have their basic human rights snatched away as per an arrangement that has its roots in religious texts. Throughout history, there have been several anti-caste movements, assertions and literatures which focused on bringing changes in the socio-economic position of Dalits and the abolition of caste oppression. However, caste continues to be a factor in India's economy and polity, and caste-based violence and agitations have gone up in the past couple of years. Dalit and Adivasi communities are subjected to inequality and discrimination even to this day, and this reality manifests in different forms. They still lag behind other caste groups in most socio-economic criteria. The below poverty line (BPL) percentage among SCs was 31.5 per cent in rural areas and 21.7 per cent in urban areas in 2011–12.[9]

Discrimination, exclusion, inequality and the system of untouchability based on caste continues to operate and thrive in the country. Despite formal legal protection by law, discriminatory norms continue to be reinforced by state and non-state actors, often through violence. There are very strong caste divisions between Dalits and other caste groups in aspects like housing, religious practices, employment and marriage, among many others. The incidence of violence against Dalits has not shown a decline and remains persistent in different forms like murder, rape, physical assault, verbal abuse and so on and so forth. Cases of violence against women, particularly Dalit women, are even more atrocious. As per National Crime Records Bureau (NCRB) data, 2016 witnessed 2541 reported cases of rape and 3172 cases of assault on Dalit women with an intent to outrage modesty.[10] There have been several attacks by extremist Hindu groups over wide-ranging issues such as beef-eating and inter-caste marriage, and lynching of Dalits and Adivasis, exhibiting a growing culture of communal extravagance. These communities are forced to live with constant fear of abhorrence and violence.

The following figure indicates an upsurge in cases of violence against SCs and STs as per the NCRB.

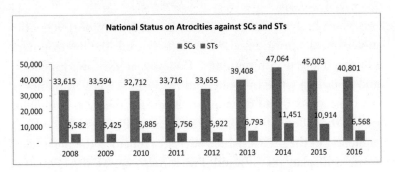

Source: National Crime Records Bureau

Exclusion and discrimination is visible not only in civic and political spheres but also in the economic arena, particularly in terms of occupation, labour employment and market arrangement. 'In the market economy framework, occupational immobility would operate through restrictions in various markets such as land, labour, credit, other inputs, and services necessary for any economic activity. Labour being an integral part of the production process of any economic activity would obviously become a part of market discrimination,' write Newman and Thorat.[11] Dalits are often restricted to particular kinds of occupations that are often considered 'polluted', with low wages and very little options for mobility. Manual scavenging is one of the definitive examples that reflects their economic position in the labour market. Based on caste hierarchy, Dalits make up the majority of manual scavengers in the country, with Dalit women being seen in huge numbers. The entrenched concept of pollution and discrimination connected with manual scavenging makes it difficult for them to find any alternative livelihood opportunities, pushing them into the age-old vicious circle of poverty and exclusion. It is sad to note that over the last few years the deaths of sewage workers have increased, with 634 deaths related to manual scavenging recorded in the last twenty-five years.[12]

The budget is a document that demonstrates the government's priorities and its efforts towards the development of marginalized communities. Looking at the discrimination and exclusion faced by Dalits and Adivasis, the government has over the years made certain provisions for their development, one of them being the Special Component Plan for SCs and STs launched in the 1970s, which was later renamed the Scheduled Caste Sub-plan (SCSP) and Tribal Sub-plan (TSP). This was introduced as a mechanism particularly for the economic empowerment of Dalits and Adivasis. These allocations are meant for umbrella programmes under which various schemes implemented by the government need to be dovetailed for the diverse needs of SCs. The funds earmarked for SCSP are placed under separate budget heads/sub-heads by each ministry or department.[13] However, in recent years, there has been a policy-level change that has negatively impacted the sub-plan. There has been a shift from a rights-based approach towards a welfare approach, which is a clear regressive step, making SCs mere beneficiaries of welfare programmes. The allocation of funds under SCSP and TSP for the last four years clearly indicates the government's lack of will in the economic empowerment of the community. Not a single year has seen the allocation of SCSP and TSP as per the population percentage of SC and ST communities. There is a serious denial of equitable allocations because of which many schemes that directly benefit SCs and STs are facing a fund crunch.[14]

Analysis of SC and ST Budgets[15]

Analysis of the Union budget for the last five financial years reveals that the powerful targeted budgeting of the SCSP and TSP has been demoted and brought down from being a policy-driven budgetary measure to a mere executing direction being issued by the Ministry of Finance. In addition, there has been under-allocation towards SCs and STs across the years. The initial two years of allocations in the table are before the merger of plan and non-plan budget expenditure, that is, FY 2015–16 to FY 2016–17. During these two years, the allocation trends appear as though they are increasing: 26 per cent for SCs from FY 2015–16 to FY 2016–17. During these two years, the total plan outlay was Rs 10,15,287 crore for SCs, of which the total allocation was Rs 69,684 crore, which accounts as 6.86 per cent. Similarly, for STs in the same period, the allocation trends are also found to be increasing, by 20 per cent from FY 2015–16 to FY 2016–17. During these two years, the total allocation was Rs 44,005 crore, which constitutes 4.27 per cent as compared to the due share of Rs 87,315 crore (8.6 per cent) for STs. The allocation is further narrowed if we look at the nature of the allocation of funds—direct allocation and general allocation. This will be discussed under 'The Nature of the Allocation' later in the essay.

As per the new guidelines issued by the Ministry of Finance, the fund will be earmarked for SCs and STs from the pool of schemes comprising Central Sector (CS) and Centrally Sponsored Schemes (CSS). This is a shift away from the earlier policy of mandating ministries/departments to allocate funds. From now on, the allocation is based on the proportion of amounts allocated to the schemes for SCs and STs. The ministries have been divided into four categories, each with a specific proportion to be allocated for SCs and STs. As per the current policy outlined by the Ministry of Finance, the total eligible CS + CSS funding for FY 2019–20 is Rs 9,51,334 crore. The due allocation is of Rs 1,41,309 crore, for which the allocated amount under the SC budget is Rs 81,341 crore.

Analysis of the period from FY 2017–18 to FY 2019–20 reveals that only Rs 1,90,352 crore has been disbursed for the development schemes for SCs and Rs 1,23,939 crore for the development schemes for STs. A total Rs 2,66,964 crore is denied towards SC development and Rs 1,34,072 crore denied for ST development as far as total gaps in allocation are concerned. In addition to the gaps in the allocation stage for SCs and STs, the quantitative analysis reveals that over the last five years the total expenditure of the Union government has been found to be increasing but the allocation towards the development of SCs and STs is found to be negligible.

Budget for Scheduled Castes—Five-Year Trend Analysis of Union Budgets FYs 2015–20 (Rs crore)

Financial Year	Total Plan Outlay/ CS+CSS Schemes (A)	Due Allocations[16] (B)	Allocation Earmarked (Statement 10A of Budget Estimate BE) [C]	Proportion of Allocation to SC Schemes (C% to A) [D]	Gap in Allocation: SC [B-C] [E]	Total Targeted Schemes: SC [F]	Total Non-Targeted Schemes: SC [G]	Total Gap: SC (G+E)
2015–16 (BE)	4,65,277	77,236	30,851	6.63%	46,385	9121	21,730	68,115
2016–17 (BE)	5,50,010	91,302	38,833	7.06%	52,469	6665	32,168	84,637
2017–18 (BE)	5,88,025	97,612	52,393	8.91%	45,220	25,708	26,685	71,904
2018–19 (BE)	7,88,395	1,17,282	56,619	7.18%	60,663	28,698	27,921	88,584
2019–20 (BE)	9,51,334	1,41,309	81,341	8.55%	59,968	34,833	46,507	1,06,475
Total	**33,43,041**	**5,24,740**	**2,60,035**	**7.67%**	**2,64,705**	**1,05,025**	**1,55,010**	**4,19,715**

Source: Union Budget Expenditure Profile, 2015–16 to 2019–20

Budget for Scheduled Tribes—Five-Year Trend Analysis of Union Budget FYs 2015–20 (Rs crore)

Financial Year	Total Plan Outlay/ CS+CSS Schemes (A)	Due Allocations[17] (B)	ST Allocation Earmarked (Statement 10B of BE) [C]	Proportion of Allocation to ST Schemes (C% to A) [D]	Gap in Allocation: ST [B-C] [E]	Total Targeted Schemes: ST [F]	Total Non-targeted Schemes: ST [G]	Total Gap: ST (G+E)
2015–16 (BE)	4,65,277	40,014	20,000	4.30%	20,014	7469	12,531	32,545
2016–17 (BE)	5,50,010	47,301	24,005	4.36%	23,295	8791	15,215	38,510
2017–18 (BE)	5,88,025	50,570	31,920	5.43%	18,651	15,643	16,276	34,927
2018–19 (BE)	7,84,881	64,486	39,135	4.99%	25,351	19,623	19,512	44,863
2019–20 (BE)	9,47,228	76,592	52,885	5.58%	23,707	21,628	31,257	54,964
Total	33,27,500	2,78,281	1,67,944	5.02%	1,10,337	73,154	94,791	2,05,128

Source: Union Budget Expenditure Profile, 2015–16 to 2019–20

The Nature of the Allocation[18]

In addition to the under-allocation, there is a huge proportion of allocation for non-direct funds which hardly reaches the targeted beneficiaries. Majority of the large quantum allocations in SC and ST schemes are general in nature with no direct impact on their development. A deeper analysis of the nature of allocation under SC funds reveals that in FY 2019–20, the total fund allocation for SC development was Rs 81,341 crore, out of which the targeted fund was only Rs 34,833 crore, which accounts for 43 per cent, and Rs 46,507 crore for non-targeted schemes, which accounts for 57 per cent. Similarly, the total fund allocation for ST development is Rs 52,885 crore, of which the targeted allocation is Rs 21,628 crore, which accounts for 41 per cent of the total Scheduled Tribe Component Plan (STCP) fund.

Furthermore, the total fund allocation over the last five years is Rs 2,60,035 crore for SCs, of which the direct fund[19] is Rs 1,05,025 crore, which accounts for 40 per cent, and the non-direct fund is Rs 1,55,010 crore, which accounts for 60 per cent. Similarly, the total fund allocation for STs over the last five years is Rs 1,67,944 crore, of which the direct fund is Rs 73,154 crore, which accounts for 44 per cent. The non-direct fund is Rs 94,791 crore, which accounts for 56 per cent. A total of Rs 2,05,128 crore has been denied to ST communities over the last five years.

The majority of the huge allocations which are allocated in sub-plans are general in nature. For example, under the SC and ST budget, the Income Support Scheme (renamed as Pradhan Mantri Kisan Samman Nidhi) with an allocation of Rs 18,900 crore, which includes Rs 12,450 crore for SCs and Rs 6450 crore for STs; the Samagra Shiksha Abhiyan with an allocation of Rs 11,496 crore (Rs 7264 crore for SCs and Rs 4232 crore for STs), and the National Rural Health Mission with an allocation of Rs 9926 crore (Rs 6611 crore for SCs and Rs 3314 crore for STs) are all general in nature. There are also obsolete schemes which are not relevant to the community and are completely notional in nature like 'Improvement in Salary Scale of University and College Teachers' and 'Compensation to Service Providers for Creation and Augmentation of Telecom Infrastructure, Bharatnet'. In FY 2019–20, out of fifty-two major schemes, there are twenty-six general schemes amounting to Rs 69,065 crore and twelve obsolete schemes amounting to Rs 8189 crore.

Budget Expenditure[20]

Actual expenditure (AE) is considered to be one of the authentic figures in the budget document that is provided by the independent audit department and published by the Ministry of Finance. There has been a severe underutilization of funds for SCs and STs, which is revealed by the four-year trends. In FY 2014–15, the approved budget under the Scheduled Caste Component (SCC) was Rs 50,548 crore, of which the utilized amount was Rs 30,035 crore—resulting in an unutilized amount of Rs 20,513 crore. Similarly, under the STC fund in FY 2014–15, the allocation was Rs 32,387 crore, of which the utilization was Rs 19,921 crore—as a result of which the unutilized funds were Rs 12,466 crore. This multilevel denial of due budgetary share to SCs and STs has a huge impact on their overall development.[21]

Potential Budgets for Tackling COVID-19

This crisis has brought under deep scrutiny the inadequacy of the public healthcare system in the country. It is to be noted that only about 1.28 per cent of the total GDP is allocated for public health, which is a pittance compared to the total population of the country. There has to be a serious revamp of the healthcare system as well as calculated measures to ensure that public health is considered a right and all people, irrespective of caste or class, have equal access to quality healthcare. Although the government has announced measures, both monetary and otherwise, to handle this crisis, there are no special mechanisms to address the issues of disempowered sections of society. One impact of the lockdown has been that several families are struggling to make ends meet and also facing starvation. Immediate and urgent actions are required to tackle this problem. Apart from the PM Cares fund and private donors, there are also allocations under several schemes that are already in Budget 2020–21—Rs 343 crore been allocated for the National Food Security Mission under the SC budget. The government should ensure that all poor SC households have food security during this prolonged lockdown period.

Limitations from the Supply and Demand Side

From the experiences of Dalit rights NGOs and community-based organizations like the National Campaign on Dalit Human Rights (NCDHR) across the years, there is a realization that change takes place when there are efforts from both the supply and demand sides to ensure transparency and accountability. To improve the community's participation in the budget, it becomes absolutely necessary to involve them in the budgetary process by mobilizing and capacitating them. It is through the enabling of the community to be active partners and to proactively engage in the planning and implementation of public entitlements that this diversion of funds and schemes meant for Dalit and Adivasi welfare and development will get more effectively implemented. There have been certain limitations in this regard both from the demand and supply side. Some of these critical gaps have been addressed below.

Firstly, Dalit and Adivasi budgets are being diverted to other sectors and purposes, and funds are instead being used for general expenditure. The large diversion during the 2010 Commonwealth Games is one such case, for which Rs 744 crore from the SCSP budget was used. The NCDHR, along with the Housing and Land Rights Network, studied the Delhi government's SC budget allocations and established that SC funds were being diverted to the Commonwealth Games. This news gathered a lot of media attention, as a result of which it was assured that the diverted amount would be returned to the Scheduled Caste Component Plan. Around Rs 540 crore was given back to the Delhi government SC budget pool.

Secondly, even these limited funds which are channelled to SCs and STs through component plans are not certain. A large proportion of their funds is allocated towards general programmes and schemes which are not specially designed for SCs and STs. Many ministries and departments make huge amounts of 'notional' allocations in the Union budget, which are mere paper figures and do not flow through special schemes directly benefiting SCs or STs.[22]

Thirdly, emphasis only on survival schemes, without 'targeted schemes' for the development, participation and social protection of SCs and STs, perpetuate inequalities rather than pave the way for bridging the development gap. Most of the direct benefit schemes are for survival, and not for empowerment.

Fourthly, there remain critical administrative bottlenecks in the implementation of development programmes and schemes. Appropriate budgetary norms are not being followed, and sufficient administrative, executive and accountability mechanisms to ensure the proper use of funds meant for SCs and STs are not in place in states and districts. The allocations themselves are not binding, which means these funds are under-allocated and underutilized.

Lastly, poor service delivery mechanism in the field is a serious constraint to attaining development outcomes, as the amounts for the schemes are not released on time and beneficiaries are not properly identified.

It is in the light of these challenges that Dalit rights groups have been instrumental in bridging the implementation gaps that exist within the SC and ST component plans. We have been able to contribute significantly to evidence building, making visible the gaps between stated policy and practice, strengthening public demand for the effective implementation of policies, holding the state accountable, and engaging at the policy level, which has brought some necessary changes. These interventions have led to some positive outcomes, as seen in Andhra Pradesh and Karnataka, which have adopted a fresh set of guidelines as legislation— giving further strength to the communities in ensuring effective implementation of the special component plans. Furthermore, continuous advocacy has led to the opening of a budget code (minor head code '789' by the Delhi government) followed by the national level-opening of the budget code 789, which has brought more transparency in the budgeting process pertaining to the component plans. Consistent advocacy and monitoring of budgetary allocations and some degree of accountability have made small dents in the funds being reclaimed by communities.

Additionally, there have also been certain challenges at the demand side in terms of people's participation and engagement in the budgetary process. One of the major challenges is that there is a lack of awareness among the community members regarding the several public entitlements available to them. There is also a lack of participation of people in the budgetary process across the country. Lack of necessary documents for accessing the schemes is another major issue. Moreover, the process for accessing these schemes is usually very tedious and lengthy, which discourages people from accessing these entitlements.

It is in this context that some Dalit rights groups have been consistently working towards increasing the community's involvement in the budget-making process. Putting forward the people's budget, mobilizing and capacitating the community on the budgets are some of the tactics towards attempting to change the existing norms and discourses which will help the community to effectively participate in scheme designing and also its implementation. Following are some of the suggestions that need to be considered to effectively use the fiscal policies and budgetary measures meant for SCs and STs.

Moreover, the situation post COVID-19 will be quite different from anything that the world has ever faced before, and each country will have to recalibrate how it functions to ensure that policies are people-friendly. There needs to be a boost in the livelihood and developmental component for SCs and STs. New innovative schemes for skill enhancement, entrepreneurship development and rural development schemes like horticulture are critical.

1) *Stimulus package to address the COVID-19 situation:*

    a. Stimulus package for unemployment aid for all migrant workers who are out of work

    b. Special packages for development of livelihood, land, skill enhancement and entrepreneurship development for SCs and STs affected by the lockdown

    c. Special fund for protection and development of SC and ST women

    d. PPE to be made available to all frontline workers including cleaners, manual scavengers and waste-pickers.

2) *Legislation on SC/ST budget:* The policy of allocations and utilization of funds for the welfare and development of SCs

and STs is excellent and appropriate for bridging the gap between them and the rest of the population. However, there are issues in the domain of implementation as there is no legislative framework. It is critical that this be legislated and machinery established not only to bridge the gap but also for ensuring financial inclusion.

3) *Strict guidelines*: The previous guidelines for SCSP and TSP had outlined that the schemes in which sub-plan funds are earmarked should have a clear strategy of how benefits could directly reach SC and ST individuals, areas or households/communities. It is critical that this objective of ensuring direct benefits for SC and ST communities should be spelt out in the programme designing and planning with a clear directive in the new guidelines.

4) *Creation of a central pool*: A central non-lapsable pool of SCC and STC funds must be created to deposit the unspent money, and a plan designed to implement new schemes which will be directly beneficial to the SC and ST population.

5) *Innovative schemes*: Schemes for the socio-economic rehabilitation of survivors of atrocities, which includes their families (such as the Nirbhaya Fund for survivors of sexual assault) are necessary, and these should provide housing, livelihood support, education facilities and safety, including free legal aid, to survivors.

6) *Manual scavenging*: The allocation for the Self-Employment Scheme for Rehabilitation of Manual Scavengers should be increased and adequate schemes provided to ensure that this practice is totally eliminated. Adequate mechanisms should be in place to monitor and track the effective use of funds.

7) *Education justice*: The arrears/unspent amount which was assured by the Department of Higher Education in the previous financial year, 2018–19, should be released. The

funds allocated for the Post Matric Scholarship and other University Grants Commission (UGC) schemes need to be disbursed in a timely manner so that students can avail the scholarships in time to complete their studies. Adequate budgetary allocation is needed to meet the demand from students belonging to the SC and ST communities who would like to pursue their higher education in universities abroad. Funds should also be allocated for high-quality residential schools for SC and ST children.

8) *Gender budget*: Direct schemes catering to SC and ST women should be increased. A special component for Dalit and Adivasi women should be allocated within the SCC and STC. Also, the inclusion of transgender persons in the SCC and STC is critical.

9) *Access to justice*: The latest NCRB report for the year 2017 should be released. Adequate budgetary allocations are needed to ensure that both punitive and pecuniary measures are in place to prevent the high incidences of violence and atrocities that are taking place on Dalits and Adivasis. Special courts for the speedy trial of cases related to the Dalit and Adivasi communities are also needed. Increased compensation amounts need to be given to victims of caste- and ethnicity-based atrocities.

10) *Planning with the community*: For the new ministries which will now earmark allocations under the sub-plans, there need to be new schemes planned and designed for providing direct benefits to the SC and ST communities.

In the current sociopolitical environment where COVID-19 has changed the very face of this country, voices of dissent are being increasingly silenced. The situation has multiplied the vulnerabilities of Dalits and will lead to absolute poverty and exclusion, further aggravated by the apathy of elected representatives. As the fight against the pandemic takes top priority, holding the state accountable has taken a back seat. It is but obvious that there will continue to be more barriers in accessing justice, both pecuniary and penal. Issues related to governance and accountability will continue to haunt marginalized communities as more and more stringent laws are being proposed to silence people's voices even as the fight against COVID-19 continues.

The Role of Independent Institutions in Protecting and Promoting Constitutional Rights

Prashant Bhushan and Anjali Bharadwaj

Independent, impartial and effective institutions are the guarantors of the rule of law on which a democratic republic is founded. Robust institutions ensure that the rule of law is not overwhelmed by the weight of numbers in a democracy. They protect citizens against the arbitrary use of power by the state and its functionaries.

In India, people have fought for, and secured, a slew of legislations that have granted them rights, including the right to information, employment, education and food security. Apart from enabling citizens, particularly the most marginalized and historically deprived, to individually and collectively assert their share in economic resources, these rights have the potential to facilitate democratic engagement with the state.

It has, however, become increasingly clear that the formal promulgation of a set of substantive rights alone is not sufficient. In order to become effective, rights require a network of supporting institutions. Experience in India has shown that creating, populating and sustaining these institutions needed to make democratic rights effective is an arduous task, requiring constant public engagement.

This chapter focuses on four critical institutions in India—the judiciary, information commissions, Lokpal and the Central Bureau of Investigation (CBI). It highlights the current challenges in the way of their independent functioning that inhibit their ability to play the role expected of them.

The Judiciary

The protection of peoples' rights is closely linked to the functioning of a fair, independent and effective justice system. In the constitutional scheme, the Indian judiciary occupies a pivotal position as the guardian of the fundamental rights and liberties of individuals. It has been widely credited with pronouncing progressive judgments upholding the rights of the marginalized and the values enshrined in the Constitution. These virtues have not been absolute, however. There have been serious concerns, from time to time, regarding the subversion of the autonomy of the judiciary, including the period when Emergency was declared in the 1970s.

Recent developments have exposed deep faultlines in the Indian judiciary. In January 2018, a press conference was addressed by four senior judges of the Supreme Court. The trigger for the unprecedented step was apparently the arbitrary allocation of benches by the chief justices, with cases being 'selectively' assigned to particular judges to obtain particular outcomes.[1] The allegations raised serious doubts about the independence of the judiciary given that an estimated 45 to 70 per cent of the litigation involves the government.[2] These doubts have been further exacerbated by the handling of several politically sensitive cases by the apex court involving allegations of corruption against some of the highest functionaries in the government, such as in the Rafale deal and the Sahara–Birla diaries.[3]

In April 2019, allegations of sexual harassment surfaced against the chief justice of India (CJI).[4] The manner[5] in which the case was dealt with brought to the fore questions about the lack of any credible mechanism to examine complaints regarding misconduct by judges of the higher judiciary, especially the CJI. Immediately after the complaint was made, the CJI presided over a hearing in which he himself was a party, flouting the fundamental principle of justice that no one should be a judge in his/her own cause. The complainant was publicly maligned, and in violation of the principles of natural justice, was not even given an opportunity to be heard. After massive public outrage, an inquiry was set up to look into the matter, though the way in which it was conducted foreclosed the opportunity for justice to prevail. The report on the basis of which the complaint was finally dismissed was never provided to the complainant![6]

When allegations of financial corruption surfaced against a previous CJI, in the medical college case,[7] the matter was similarly dismissed with little regard for established procedures and principles. In that case, not only did the Supreme Court dismiss the plea for a court-monitored probe by a Special Investigation Team (SIT), but also held it to be contemptuous and imposed costs on the petitioner organization.

The inability of the judiciary to provide a robust and credible system for looking into allegations of misconduct by judges seriously erodes public trust and confidence in the institution. Despite glaring loopholes in the existing procedures,[8] including the fact that there is no effective mechanism in place to receive and act on complaints of misconduct against the CJI, the judiciary has taken no steps to rectify them.

Perhaps one way in which the judiciary could have infused greater accountability in its functioning without compromising its independence was by being transparent. The judiciary has played a seminal role in recognizing and furthering the people's right to information. Unfortunately, even after the passage of the Right to Information (RTI) Act in 2005, which is also applicable to the judiciary, experience suggests that the courts have not been forthcoming in providing information about their own functioning under the law.[9]

Many RTI applications filed by citizens seeking information from the courts have themselves required judicial adjudication. These include information requests about records related to the appointment of judges, declarations of assets held by judges, cases pending with the apex court in which arguments had already been heard but judgments had been reserved, and correspondence between the then CJI and a judge of the Madras High Court regarding the attempt of a Union minister to influence judicial decisions of the said high court.[10] By resisting transparency in its functioning, the judiciary has evaded its accountability to the people of India.

Opaqueness in the process of judicial appointments has been a matter of intense public debate over the years. The 2015 judgment[11] of the Supreme Court in the National Judicial Appointments Commission (NJAC) matter underlined the need to enhance transparency in the functioning of the collegium system. The refusal of Justice Jasti Chelameswar to attend meetings of the collegium on the grounds that its functioning lacks transparency,[12] with even some members of the collegium not being informed of the basis on which judicial appointments are made, pointed to the deep malaise that afflicts the judicial appointment process. Though some measures have been taken recently to place resolutions of the collegium in the public domain, the memorandum of procedure related to the appointment of judges continues to be kept under covers.

The resistance to transparency in judicial appointments is inexplicable, given that in numerous cases, the Supreme Court itself ordered that appointments must be made in a transparent manner on the basis of rational criteria, which are appropriately recorded.

One of the methods the present government has used to control the judiciary is the manner in which appointments and transfers of judges to the higher judiciary are being done. The government has effectively stalled the process of judicial appointments by not notifying the appointment of judges recommended by the collegium to various high courts and to the Supreme Court, even when the recommendations are reiterated by the collegium.[13] This is contrary to the settled law on judicial appointments to the higher judiciary. The apex court in the *Supreme Court Advocates-on-Record Association v. Union of India*[14] (second judges' case) had held that once a recommendation has been reiterated by the CJI with the unanimous agreement of the judges of the collegium, with reasons for not withdrawing the recommendation, then that appointment ought to be notified by the government. The executive in such a situation would be bound by the final opinion of the collegium. The courts have also held that compliance with a time-bound schedule for judicial appointments is essential to maintain the integrity of the appointment process. Non-adherence to a time-bound schedule and the adoption of dilatory tactics by the executive results in the stalling of the appointment of various judges to high courts and to the Supreme Court. Sitting on the proposed recommendations and delaying the process of judicial appointments has an adverse effect on not just the appointment process but also the independence of the judiciary.

A critical power that can be wielded by the CJI is to be a prime mover in the appointment of judges. Unfortunately, several chief justices have not pushed the matter with the government by issuing a mandamus on the judicial side or hauling up the government for contempt. Perhaps this reluctance is a result of pressure exerted by the executive on judges through the use of investigative agencies or due to the lure of post-retirement jobs.[15]

The role of the judiciary is critical for the realization of all rights since the judiciary is ultimately the institution where people can seek redress for injustices they have suffered, particularly if other channels of seeking such redress have failed. The lack of transparency and accountability in the functioning of the judiciary erodes public trust in the institution and ultimately hampers its ability to uphold democratic principles and deliver justice.

Information Commissions

Through various pronouncements, the courts have held that the right to information is a fundamental right flowing from Article 19 and Article 21 of the Constitution, and that transparency in the working of public authorities is critical in a democracy.

The RTI Act has empowered Indians to question governments and has initiated the critical task of redistributing power in a democratic framework. With more than six million information applications filed every year,[16] the Indian RTI Act is the most extensively used transparency legislation globally. The law has been used extensively by people on a range of issues—from holding the government accountable for the delivery of basic rights and entitlements to questioning the highest offices of the country.

It is perhaps this paradigm shift in the locus of power through the use of the law that has resulted in consistent efforts by the powerful to denigrate it. There have been consistent attacks on the institution of information commissions, which adjudicate on the appeals and complaints of citizens who have been denied access to information under the sunshine law.

The central and state governments have realized that an effective way of curbing access to information that is inconvenient and embarrassing for governments to disclose is to undermine the functioning of information commissions. As per the RTI Act, the appointment of commissioners in the Central Information Commission is made by a committee comprising the prime minister (chairperson), a cabinet minister and the leader of the single largest Opposition party in the Lok Sabha, while in states, the appointments are made by the chief minister, a cabinet minister and the leader of the Opposition in the Assembly. Governments have impeded the functioning of information commissions by not filling vacancies in posts of information commissioners in a timely manner. Vacancies lead to large backlogs of appeals/complaints and concomitant long delays in the disposal of these cases. A report[17] published in October 2019 found that eleven information commissions had a waiting time of more than one year for cases to be disposed, with some taking more than five years![18] While hearing a matter regarding the non-appointment of information commissioners and the lack of transparency in the appointments, the Supreme Court in its judgment[19] in early 2019 observed that the failure of governments to appoint commissioners was 'negating the very purpose for which this Act came into force'. The track record of the current central government, which came to power on the plank of good governance, has been particularly poor. Since May 2014, not a single commissioner of the Central Information Commission has been appointed without citizens having to approach courts.[20]

Further, appointments of information commissioners are often made in an arbitrary, non-transparent manner, with mainly retired public servants being appointed in the position.[21] In many states, including Gujarat, Andhra Pradesh and Kerala, the appointments of information commissioners have been set aside by courts due to the lack of transparency in the process of their appointment, or because persons who did not meet the eligibility criteria were appointed as commissioners. Despite the law clearly stating that commissioners should be persons of eminence in public life with wide knowledge and experience from diverse backgrounds, since the RTI law came into effect, an overwhelming majority of chief information commissioners (83 per cent) and information commissioners (nearly 60 per cent) have been appointed from among retired civil servants.[22] Even the Supreme Court of India[23] has commented on the phenomenon of primarily former bureaucrats being appointed as commissioners, observing that 'it is difficult to fathom that persons belonging to one category only are always found to be more competent and more suitable than persons belonging to other categories'.

The functioning of information commissions themselves has been far from satisfactory. Assessments[24] have shown that commissioners often deny information in violation of the law and are reluctant to use their powers to penalize officials who violate the law, with penalties imposed in only 4.1 per cent of the cases where they were imposable.

In July 2019, the RTI Act was amended to undermine the autonomy of information commissions.[25] The amendments empowered the central government to make rules to determine the tenure, salaries, allowances and other terms of service of all information commissioners in the country. The RTI Act of 2005 fixed the tenure of information commissioners at five years, subject to the retirement age of sixty-five years. Further, the salaries, allowances and other terms of service of the chief of the Central Information Commission was pegged at the same level as that of the chief election commissioner. Those of the central information commissioners and state chief commissioners were on par with election commissioners. The chief and other election commissioners are paid a salary equal to the salary of a judge of the Supreme Court, which is decided by Parliament.

The fixed tenure and high status conferred on commissioners under the RTI Act was to empower them to carry out their functions autonomously, without fear or favour, and direct even the highest offices to comply with the provisions of the law. Empowering the central government to decide the tenure and terms of service of information commissioners compromises their independence; directions to disclose inconvenient information could invite adverse consequences from the central government.

Undermining the Lokpal

The Lokpal law was enacted as a result of a strong public campaign demanding the setting up of an empowered and independent institution to tackle cases of corruption, which rob millions of people of their basic rights and services. The preambular statement of the Lokpal and Lokayuktas Act, 2013 (L&L Act), notes that the law is being enacted to ensure prompt and fair investigation and prosecution in cases of corruption.

Although the law came into force on 16 January 2014 through notification in the Official Gazette, the institution of the Lokpal was not made operational until 2019. The chairperson and members of the Lokpal were appointed in 2019, more than five years after the law was enacted, in a manner that raised serious questions about the credibility[26] of the selection process.

An important principle for ensuring the independence of bodies such as the Lokpal is that the selection committee responsible for making appointments to these institutions should not have a preponderance of representatives of the government and the ruling party. The L&L Act provides for the appointment of the chairperson and members of the Lokpal by the President based on the recommendations of a committee consisting of the prime minister (chairperson), the Speaker of the House of the People, the leader of the Opposition in the House of the People, the CJI or a judge of the Supreme Court nominated by him/her, and an eminent jurist, as recommended by the chairperson and other members.

After the 2014 general elections, no one was recognized as the leader of the Opposition in the Lok Sabha. In order to ensure a balanced selection committee in keeping with the spirit of the legislation, the government needed to bring a single amendment to modify the composition of the selection committee by substituting the recognized leader of the Opposition with the leader of the single largest Opposition party in the Lok Sabha. The government introduced a ten-page amendment bill in December 2014, which instead of limiting itself to amending the composition of the selection committee, sought to fundamentally dilute the original law. Given the controversial nature of amendments, the bill was never enacted.

The matter of non-appointment of the Lokpal was agitated in the Supreme Court.[27] The Court held that appointments could be made with a truncated selection committee without the leader of the Opposition. Despite the ruling of the Supreme Court, the government did not initiate the appointment process leading to a contempt petition[28] being filed in the apex court in January 2018. Finally, the selection committee headed by Prime Minister Narendra Modi met for the first time in March 2018, nearly forty-five months after the BJP formed the government.

The PM, the Speaker and the CJI appointed Mukul Rohatgi, who served as attorney general during the BJP regime, as the eminent jurist on the selection panel. In the absence of the leader of the Opposition, the selection of the chairperson and members of the Lokpal came under a cloud, with doubts arising about an inherent bias towards the selection of candidates favoured by the government. The then leader of the largest Opposition party in the Lok Sabha was invited to the meetings of the selection committee as a 'special invitee'. He declined[29] the invite on the grounds that a special invitee 'would not have any rights of participation in the process of selection'.

Sub-section 4 of Section 4 of the L&L Act mandates that the selection committee should regulate its own procedure in a transparent manner. Transparency in the functioning of the selection panel could have helped allay fears that the committee was merely rubber-stamping the government's choice of candidates. However, the functioning of the committee was shrouded in secrecy and no details of the selection process were placed in the public domain.

The composition of the selection committee and the lack of transparency in the selection process by which the chair and members of the Lokpal were finally appointed in March 2019 have raised doubts about the ability of the Lokpal to function independently and perform its role effectively.

Central Bureau of Investigation

The CBI, established under the Delhi Special Police Establishment Act (DSPE), 1946, is the premier investigation agency in the country.

Unfortunately, political interference in the functioning of the CBI has been rife, resulting in the derailment of justice in a vast number of cases, especially those that are politically sensitive. The apex court has referred to the institution as a 'caged parrot',[30] and in its landmark judgment in the *Vineet Narain* case[31] in 1997 gave specific directions to insulate the CBI from extraneous influence. Specifically, the Court instructed that the director of the CBI should have full freedom to allocate work in the organization, including the constitution of investigation teams. It gave detailed directions related to the appointment of the director of the CBI. Further, in order to eliminate ad hocism in the appointment and functioning of the CBI director and to ensure independence, the Court ruled that the CBI director should have a fixed tenure of two years.

Subsequently, amendments were made to the DSPE Act, first in 2003 vide the Central Vigilance Commission Act, and again in 2013 through the L&L Act, to insulate the selection committee from government influence. The appointment of the CBI director under the amended law has to be made by the central government on the recommendation of the prime minister, the leader of the single largest Opposition party in the Lok Sabha, and the CJI (or any judge of the Supreme Court nominated by the CJI). Further, the law now provides for a fixed tenure of two years, and the director can be transferred only with the prior consent of the high-powered selection committee.

In October 2018, however, in blatant violation of the law, vide two separate orders issued by the Central Vigilance Commission and the Government of India, the then director of the CBI, Alok Verma, was divested of his powers, and M. Nageswara Rao was made the director as an interim measure. These orders were challenged on the grounds that the government acted unilaterally and bypassed the high-powered selection committee in complete contravention of the established procedure.

In its judgment[32] dated 8 January 2019, the Supreme Court quashed both orders, but serious questions arose about the autonomy of the investigating agency and the control exercised by the executive on its functioning.

The Way Forward

Autonomous and robust institutions are the bedrock of a democracy, without which peoples' rights are liable to be trampled with impunity. They can stand as bulwarks against the dangers that threaten democracies.

To enable institutions to function autonomously, it is critical that appointments to them be made in a timely manner by a balanced selection committee which does not have majority representation from the ruling party. The committee must adopt a transparent appointment process mandating public disclosure of particulars of applicants, shortlisting criteria, records of deliberations, including minutes of meetings of the selection committee and material showing how the selected candidates fulfil the eligibility criteria.

To empower them to function without fear or favour, it is important that the tenure, salaries and terms of service of their officials not be determined by the executive. Transfers and removals should be done by a committee that does not have a preponderance of the government.

Proper mechanisms of accountability for all functionaries of institutions are key to ensuring that they work in the interest of the people. One of the most effective ways to make institutions accountable to the people in a democracy is to infuse transparency in their functioning and open them to public scrutiny.

Rights-Based Development and Democratic Decentralization in Kerala

T.M. Thomas Isaac and S.M. Vijayanand

Powerful currents of popular demand from below and actions taken by responsive governments, even from the colonial period, have characterized the development experience of Kerala. Redistributive measures—such as land reforms, collective bargaining for higher wages and public provisioning of education, healthcare, food and social security and so on—ensured that the average citizen is assured of the basic needs that uphold human dignity. Social reform movements, particularly those focused on education as the liberating force, triggered changes in related sectors. There were regular 'petitions', 'memorials' to the rulers and even popular protests and agitations, and the state was mostly accommodating and met many a demand halfway. Access to government schools and hospitals was given to all sections of society, even in the first quarter of the twentieth century. Rights-consciousness among the backward classes, inculcated by social reform initiatives, enabled them to fully utilize these opportunities. The powerful social movements also began to weaken the rabid and primitive caste system which had made Swami Vivekananda describe Kerala as a 'lunatic asylum'.[1]

Progressive mass organizations and political parties took forward the inclusive agenda and deepened the rights-consciousness that already existed. The first four decades after Independence were characterized by potent and effective mass struggles demanding the right to land, food, decent wages, education, health and social security. Successive governments had to respond positively to these demands, giving shape to an inclusive system of governance and development. In addition to health and education, land reforms were given special priority. Land reforms resulted in the transferring and formalizing of ownership rights to the tenant and incorporating a right to homestead for the landless poor, most of whom largely belonged to the SC category.

Universal food security was operationalized way back in the mid-1960s. Kerala has also been a pioneer in social security, especially in creating welfare funds for labour groups. Today, nearly 50 lakh persons, including the disabled, widows and the aged, receive a monthly pension of Rs 1200.[2] In respect of labour rights, the state adopted a pro-labour policy ensuring that the provisions of labour laws are actually implemented, putting in place an innovative tripartite mechanism for conciliation. Currently, the wage rate for rural wage labourers is more than double the national average.[3] There is universal schooling and universal primary healthcare.

Kerala is a place of vibrant democratic politics, with a strong 'organization culture' in society and polity, and almost everyone has multiple memberships in associations—political, social, religious, occupational, civic, etc. This has generated huge social capital with a rights-conscious citizenry. There have been regular demands and negotiations on different rights, and continuous defining and redefining as well as progressive enhancing of entitlements. It would not be too off the mark to state that Kerala pioneered the concept of development as a right long before it came to be discussed in the public sphere in the country.

People's Plan

Democratic decentralization holds great potential to tap the social capital of such a rights-conscious society for improving the productivity of small-scale sectors, delivery of services and attainment of basic minimum needs. Its roots may be traced to Gandhiji's emphasis on village democracy and participatory development with a focus on *antyodaya* (upliftment of the weakest sections of society). In the context of Kerala, the Marxist approach of leaders such as E.M.S. Namboodiripad, who viewed decentralization as a means to widen and deepen the parliamentary democratic system and help in the mobilization of the working people and furtherance of their rights, reinforced this. Decentralization would empower farmers in the post-land-reform era, workers in the small-scale traditional sectors who were in cooperatives, and the people dependent upon local public schools and hospitals, to improve the productivity and quality of services. This was very important in the era of globalization which posed a great threat to petty production and the danger of privatization of public services.

It was against such a background that the People's Plan was launched in August 1996. Under it, Kerala followed a 'big bang' decentralization campaign, conferring genuine powers, functions and authority, matched by more than adequate resources, upon local governments. Through this approach, it attempted a set of 'reversals' of conventional wisdom—delegating powers and then putting in systems, giving responsibilities and then building capacity, providing resources and then bringing in accountability arrangements. The process of participatory planning was utilized as an instrument of social mobilization so that people cutting across political and other divides generate an environment and will for effective decentralization.

The objectives of the People's Plan[4] included:

- Democratization and humanization of the state
- Widening and deepening participation, enabling people, especially the poor, the disempowered and women, to have a role and a say in local developmental governance
- Shifting from bureaucratic top-down planning and budgeting to participatory, bottom-up planning and budgeting with active involvement of professionals and practitioners from outside the government as volunteers
- Moving from official and political patronage to decisions based on societal norms and criteria for providing benefits to people, developed locally after discussions and debates
- Enhancing responsiveness of governance
- Increasing transparency and accountability, especially social accountability, and reducing corruption
- Transforming conflictual politics into a new politics of development responding to local demand and potential
- Facilitating cooperative and creative public action as opposed to functioning in an adversarial mode.

The Features of Democratization

The core objective of the People's Plan is widening and deepening democracy through local governments. Elections to the local governments are held on party lines but 50 per cent of the seats and positions at all levels, including standing committees, are set apart for women. The reservations for

SCs/STs are in accordance with their proportion in the population.

Elected local governments have control over the functionaries transferred to them. The principle of transfer of 'worker along with work' was adopted and implemented in full. For example, primary health is a subject under the village panchayat. Thus, the medical officer and the entire staff of the PHC, including field workers, are brought under the administrative jurisdiction of the gram panchayat, which can assign work, supervise performance, get feedback, conduct inspections and, if required, even impose minor penalties on erring staff. In order to encourage a healthy relationship between elected representatives and officials, an enforceable code of conduct has been issued as part of the statute.

The local governments of Kerala are the most autonomous in the country. They have near total freedom in deciding the application of resources transferred to them. The elected body is the executive authority. Decisions in the exercise of regulatory powers can be appealed against only to an appellate tribunal consisting of a district judge. In the case of allegations of malfeasance, citizens can approach the ombudsman, who is a current or former high court judge. Kerala is the only state in the country to have such independent institutions of accountability with no role whatsoever for the bureaucracy to sit in judgement over decisions of local governments. Even if a local government takes a decision which is wrong, the government can only stay its operation, refer it to the ombudsman and take the final decision only as per the advice of the ombudsman. If a local government is found transgressing its limits and the government feels that it should be dissolved, a chargesheet has to be framed and the local government given an opportunity to reply, after which the matter would be referred to the ombudsman. Only on the basis of this advice can the government dissolve a local government. It is noteworthy that there has not been a single such instance since 1995.

There is a very high level of 'soft' devolution in Kerala. Elected members are given special status in all public functions in their jurisdiction. Local governments have a strong identity and their members are treated with respect officially and socially. Kerala is the only state where separate local government associations exist in respect of village, block and district panchayats as well as municipalities and corporations. These bipartisan associations are given space in getting feedback on operational issues and in policy consultations, and they act as active advocacy groups.

Right at the beginning of the People's Plan, a conscious policy decision was taken to ensure that the network of the neighbourhood groups or NHGs (as self-help groups or SHGs are called in Kerala) works in close partnership with the village panchayats, municipalities and corporations. This decision was taken on the premise that if the local governments and community-based organizations of women work in parallel, as in the case of the rest of India, both would be weakened in the long run and democracy would suffer; on the other hand, if they work together in an equal relationship, the gains of democracy would multiply and lead to gains for both.

These community-based organizations of women under the Kudumbashree Mission[5] are distinct from the usual microcredit SHGs in the rest of the country. Besides microcredit, great emphasis is also given to microenterprise development. The relationship of the community-based organizations with the local governments converts them into a platform for integrating central and state programmes for poverty alleviation. They have also moved on to child rights through the organizing of Bala Sabhas. They run community-based BUDS schools for the mentally challenged. Finally, they are also seen as instruments for gender empowerment. It is also interesting to note that Kudumbashree women constitute 62.24 per cent of the elected women representatives of all local governments. Thus, a mutually beneficial relationship has emerged resulting in significant empowerment of women from the bottom half of the population.

The Spirit of Participation

Facilitating real participation of the people was one of the fundamental objectives of decentralization. Participation was conceived of not only as a means, but also as an end. For the purpose of the People's Plan, participation could be defined as 'the process by which groups hitherto excluded from development acquire the power and ability to direct resources and influence institutions meant for their well-being, in such a manner as to shape development in accordance with the needs and priorities as identified by them, and during which process their capabilities get enhanced and their entitlements extended, leading on to general public action'.[6]

Participatory planning is obviously the hallmark of Kerala's decentralization. The stages of People's Planning, as followed in Kerala, are summarized below:

1) *Situation analysis by working groups:* Working groups are set up by all local governments for different sectors. For example, a village panchayat has thirteen working groups. The composition of a working group is decided by the local government concerned; generically, it is headed by an elected representative and its member secretary is the official concerned. A respected professional is its vice chair, and its other members include stakeholders and activists. These five categories of members can see an issue from five different

perspectives and bring about what could be called 'quin-angulation'. Working groups evaluate past performance, analyse data, hold consultations and give their reports with recommendations on possible strategies and initiatives.

2) *Identification of needs:* This is done mainly in the gram sabha and ward sabha. In order to sharpen the identification of needs, stakeholder consultations are mandatory with different groups such as farmers, workers and so on. There is also a consultation with the network of SHGs, particularly in the preparation of the anti-poverty sub-plan.

3) *Development report:* All the local governments prepare development reports which are a summary of the status of development with a clear identification of problems and strategies to address them. These are prepared once in five years.

   To buttress the development reports, participatory status studies are prepared. Though not yet universalized, studies exist in respect of gender, the aged, children, the differently abled and the poorest of the poor. These have the Paulo Freiran[7] potential of self-understanding by marginalized groups, capable of setting off a process of change.

4) *Development seminar:* The next stage is validation of the priorities and strategies in consultation with representatives from gram sabhas/ward sabhas along with selected stakeholders in a development seminar.

5) *Prioritization and resource allocation:* The final prioritization and resource allocation are done by the elected local government representatives after detailed vetting in the standing committees. The rationale of the final choice and also explanation for deviation, if any, from the decisions of the development seminar are summarized in a formal plan document.

6) *Projectization:* The priorities are then converted into formal project proposals, clearly defining objectives, describing activities and time frames, undertaking simple cost–benefit analyses and gender and environment impact statements and laying out the financial outlay and sources. The quantitative dimensions of the projects are eventually digitized.

7) *Plan finalization:* After getting projects from different working groups, the plan is finalized by the elected body. This is followed by the vetting of plans, which in the first fifteen years of the People's Plan was done by committees of experts, including volunteers from outside the government. Since 2012, the vetting has been done by senior officials, which in one sense does go against the spirit of the People's Plan.

The spirit of participation is incorporated in the implementation stages also, of which an interesting feature is the process mandated for the selection of beneficiaries for different schemes. The local government has to lay down the eligibility criteria for a scheme. This is followed by fixing clear prioritization criteria which have to be given weightage in such a manner that the total comes to 100 (to facilitate easy understanding by citizens). Applications are subsequently called for, and spot inquiries conducted by committees and marks awarded. These are read out in the gram sabha/ward sabha and the selection finalized. The local government does not have the power to change this priority.

Even in the execution of works, different processes and procedures facilitate participation. Small works, limits of which are determined from time to time, could be implemented by committees of beneficiaries through a process of community contracting. Certain organizations like parent–teacher associations (PTAs) in schools are deemed to be the committee of beneficiaries for the execution of works. Some outstanding NGOs have been accredited to carry out works of local governments without going through the tender process. In the public works rules, people's estimates, that is, estimates prepared in the language of the layperson, and information boards proactively disclosing items of works and expenses are provided for.

Rights-Based Development

The People's Plan approach consciously embodied the spirit of rights-based development. Essentially, its philosophy was to enable the community to intervene formally in the identification and addressing of the root causes of different development problems by providing adequate space in policies, laws, programmes and in operational systems for such participation. As a bold antidote to the neoliberal prescription of rolling back the state, Kerala consciously followed an approach of taking the state to the doorstep of the citizen by increasing the interface and points of contact with the people and promoting a continuous to-and-fro flow of information.

The People's Plan campaign succeeded in raising the consciousness of the people on their development status and on the potential for change. It facilitated the building of capacities of the state to understand the new paradigm to enable local governments to function differently and all citizens to be aware of the new rights and opportunities.

Most of the people-related functions such as health, education, women and child development, SC/ST development, agriculture-related development, poverty alleviation, the provision of basic needs like housing, sanitation, water supply, etc. were entrusted to local governments at the cutting-edge level—village panchayats, municipalities and corporations.

Nearly 25 per cent to 30 per cent of the development budget or plan is being provided every year over the last twenty-three years to local governments in a practically untied form. Every single rupee is devolved according to a transparent formula, with zero discretion left with the state government. The formula has nearly 30 per cent weightage for backwardness, and this protection of the rights of weak and marginal local governments is an important feature in the fiscal decentralization of Kerala.

For ensuring affirmative inclusion, socially disadvantaged groups such as SCs/STs, the poorest of the poor, women, children, the aged, the differently abled, the terminally ill and now transgender people have been especially identified. To operationalize programmes for these groups, mandatory earmarking of funds is done for SCs/STs, besides setting apart 10 per cent for the women component plan and another 10 per cent for children, the aged and the differently abled. This is buttressed by process mandates such as preparation of status studies, inclusive and directly consultative planning, preparation of social maps, etc.

By law, all local governments have to prepare a citizens' charter, especially for service delivery. Social accountability is promoted through proactive disclosure through 'information boards' on the components of different programmes and public works. Though social audit has not been very successful, an informal and concurrent kind of social audit is in place, that is, the processes and systems keep people aware of what is happening. Absolute Right to Information was incorporated in the Kerala Panchayati Raj Act and Kerala Municipalities Act in 1999, six years before the central Act came into being. Several IT applications have been put in place which enhance this right. This has been further expanded by office management systems like 'front office', which enable direct citizen interface.

Performance of Local Governments and Continuing Challenges

A rapid assessment of the performance of local governments in nurturing rights-based development is in order, starting with the implementation of MGNREGA, which incorporates a 'bundle' of rights. The rights include the right to employment, right to basic social security, right to participate and decide local plans, right to equal wage, right to decent wage, right to service delivery (timely payment, basic facilities at worksites, health of workers), right to information. In combination, it is a critical step towards rights-based development.

Kerala is the only state where SHGs are directly utilized not only to assess demand, but also to organize work, with the result that more than 90 per cent of workers are women.[8] This has resulted in Kerala absorbing more than 4 per cent of MGNREGA funds even though it has only 1.93 per cent of the total population that is below the poverty line in the country. This has definitely enhanced the status of women by leaving significant savings in their hands.

As regards the right to shelter, all local governments have been giving priority to provide a house to every poor family. Not only are centrally sponsored housing schemes implemented by local governments but they are also encouraged to take loans from financial institutions, partially securitizing the future flow of grants from the state government to fast-track the provision of shelter to the needy. It is estimated that around 15 lakh houses have been built for the poor since the launch of the People's Plan. This has been proactively supported by the government.[9]

With respect to the right to education, there has been significant improvement in the last two decades in the quality of infrastructure and facilities in anganwadis and government schools. Led by effective participatory associations such as PTAs, school management committees, class PTAs and so on, every school has a master plan which presents a vision of future infrastructure of academic and co-curricular development. As a result, the trend of shrinking public education has been reversed, and the number of students in the public education system has increased substantially during the past three years.[10]

Health is another sector where there has been remarkable improvement. The local governments are important support systems for PHCs. Health indicators have witnessed significant improvement since the advent of decentralization as also the performance of government hospitals at the primary and secondary levels. The most significant development in the health sector in Kerala during the last decade has been the emergence and spread of a community-based palliative care network which has attained acclaim as an international best practice.[11]

Of late, local governments have been showing much promise in what could be described as a programme of 'care and compassion', reaching out to the destitute, mentally challenged children and differently abled. Further, local initiatives for the aged and children are indicating innovative approaches. Thus, the broader fundamental rights to equality and to life are being addressed through inclusion of the most marginalized. This is seen as an unexpected positive outcome of democratic decentralization.

As regards the right to food, the involvement of local governments in the public distribution system is marginal. But an interesting local initiative in Alappuzha by local bodies has been the provision of free food to destitute families under a scheme called 'Hunger-Free Kerala'. This has caught the attention of the state.[12]

Even though local government performance in the agriculture and small-scale industrial sector has been lacklustre, Kerala's Kudumbashree Mission is a national best practice in respect of the right to livelihood. Nearly 44 lakh families have been organized through women into nearly 3 lakh NHGs, which are federated at the level of the ward of the panchayat/municipality/ corporation into area development societies (ADSs), and further networked into community development societies (CDSs) at the level of the local government. Kudumbashree has achieved considerable success in innovative livelihood initiatives. It has brought back women into farming; as of now, 57,300 hectares have been covered through a kind of group farming by nearly 75,000 joint liability groups.[13] It has also tried out a cluster approach through a programme called 'Samagra', focusing on one economic activity in a district as per the local potential. Some of the other interesting social enterprise activities include women mason groups, women service groups of plumbers, electricians, repairpersons, etc., audit and account service groups for helping SHGs maintain proper accounts, microenterprise consultants, geriatric caregivers and so on.[14]

A major disappointment has been sanitation beyond the provision of toilets. The local governments have not been successful in creating a clean Kerala by managing solid waste satisfactorily. However, there are many exemplary local governments, such as Alappuzha Municipality, Thiruvananthapuram Corporation and Azhiyur Village Panchayat in Kozhikode district, implementing the segregation and processing of organic waste at source. Non-organic waste is sent for appropriate reuse, recycling or disposal. Efforts are on to scale up these good practices.

In respect of the right to service delivery, there are interesting experiments. Every ward in a rural area has a Gram Seva Kendra. ISO 9001:2015 certification has been obtained by all but two of the 941 village panchayats.[15]

Another noteworthy feature of Kerala's decentralization is the extraordinary levels of personal accountability on the part of the elected representatives who have to continuously respond to people's issues. This was best demonstrated when they spontaneously acted as first responders when Kerala was ravaged by massive floods in 2018 and 2019.

Though disaster management is not a function assigned to local governments, their handling of rescue and relief operations and mobilizing the community to rise to the occasion was an eye-opener. Their latest effort is leading from the front in dealing with the dreaded COVID-19 pandemic. This has attracted international acclaim as local governments have been able to play multidimensional roles in imparting humaneness in the times of lockdown, assisting health professionals in surveillance and quarantine, taking care of the aged and the sick by reaching out to them, providing food and decent care to migrants, and even watching out against hoarding, profiteering and cheating for essential commodities. It would appear that the crisis has made them realize the basic human rights of the community and grow in stature into real institutions of self-government as envisaged in the Indian Constitution.[16]

Scope for Improvement

After twenty years, there are also certain areas of concern which are being addressed in different ways, even though success is yet to be on scale. The biggest challenge is how to sustain the high level of participation. Gram sabha meetings are getting routinized with attendance largely for material benefits. Social audit is mostly perfunctory. After a remarkable dip in corruption when the People's Plan was initiated, there has been a gradual increase particularly in the execution of public works. This could partly be due to the waning participation of activists and volunteer professionals. Though it is not uncontrollable, it still needs to be addressed proactively.

The localizing of environmental rights is surprisingly weak. For example, the filling up of paddy fields, the onslaught of real-estate lobbies, sand mining, quarrying, etc. take place with impunity. Watershed-based planning still remains a distant dream. Nevertheless, local action is very important for environmental restoration, and it is one of the most severe and formidable challenges ahead of us in light of the continuing natural calamities that the state is subject to.

The integrated approach is still weak. A 'constituency mentality', resulting in the division of funds equally among wards, results in small projects and a thin spread of resources. The District Plans which were prepared were intended to bring greater coordination between the programmes of the different tiers of the local governments and the state government. But they are not yet very effective.

A sad failure has been the inability to understand and respond to the rights of tribals. There has also been criticism of inadequate response to the rights of SCs and fisherfolk. Emerging issues of the basic rights of migrant labourers working in Kerala, who number over 20 lakh, are new challenges.[17]

These and other weaknesses of democratic decentralization in Kerala should not distract from its achievements. Kerala has continuously been the top-ranked state in the index of devolution in India. It has not been affected by successive changes of state governments since the inception of the People's Plan. There is a political consensus in the state that the process should not be reversed—it has to go forward.

Conclusion

The People's Plan essentially involved a shift from top-down bureaucratic techno-managerial planning to bottom-up people-centred planning based on local needs, potential, norms and values. It contributed to the re-politicization of development in a positive sense. Rights-based approach and participatory governance are in a sense two sides of the same coin. They are linked though the concern for inclusion and social justice; both focus on defining needs and priorities by the people themselves, and participation becomes an instrument to secure entitlements and an end to sustain the achievements.

The closeness of local governments to the people provides advantages vis-à-vis the 'principles' of rights-based development:

- Universality—as local governments reach out to everyone
- Indivisibility—as local governments are in a better position to give equal importance to all rights
- Interdependence and interrelationships—as local governments are non-departmental and tend to see things holistically while responding to people's needs
- Participation and inclusion—most conducive in a local government scenario
- Accountability and rule of law—as local governments have the highest natural accountability and tend to be normative.

At the local government level, there is less of government and more of governance, a less formal and more intimate interface with citizens, and a sort of continuity between officials and citizens through the elected representatives. So there is a kind of good governance emerging from the culture of deliberations inbuilt in local governments through natural and created fora. Alliances and networks develop in relation to local government activities such as NHG networks, watershed groups, user groups and so on. As the poor can directly observe and understand how the levers of power are pulled and can be pulled, there is a kind of 'learning by observing'. This enhances community capacity development and provides space for fuller citizenship as people have more information about local government functioning and can develop a sense of playing key roles in governance.

The big lesson from Kerala is that the potential for participatory rights-based development is real and achievable in local governments. But nothing is 'per se' or 'ipso facto'; there is a need for proactive policy by the government, which has to be translated into purposive processes and procedures with active involvement, support and guidance from the fraternity of believers in democratic decentralization, inclusion and participatory development from all sections of the society.

Notes

For a Set of Universal Economic Rights

1. Karl Marx, 'On the Jewish Question' (1843), *The Marx-Engels Reader,* ed. Robert Tucker (New York: Norton & Company, 1978), pp. 26–46.
2. Amit Basole, Mathew Idiculla, Rajendran Narayanan, Harini Nagendra and Seema Mundoli, 'Strengthening Towns through Sustainable Employment: A Job Guarantee Programme for Urban India', *State of Working India Report 2019* (Bengaluru: Centre for Sustainable Employment, Azim Premji University, 2019).
3. *Report of the Education Commission 1964–66,* National Council for Educational Research and Training, 1970, http://dise.in/Downloads/KothariCommissionVol.1pp.1-287.pdf.
4. G.K. Vani, P.S. Srikantha Murthy, M. Bhattarai, 'Inter-sectoral Linkages and Multipliers of MGNREGA in a Rainfed Village in Karnataka: Applications of Social Accounting Matrix (SAM)', in M. Bhattarai, P. Viswanathan, R. Mishra, C. Bantilan, eds, *Employment Guarantee Programme and Dynamics of Rural Transformation in India* (Singapore: Springer, 2018).
5. World Economic Forum, 'Agenda in Focus: Fixing Inequality', 2019, https://www.weforum.org/focus/fixing-inequality.

6. New World Wealth, AfrAsia Bank Global Wealth Migration Review, 2019. https://e.issuu.com/embed. html?u=newworldwealth&d=gwmr_2019

Fighting Inequality: Rights and Entitlements

1. The authors would like to especially thank Ramya Ranjan Mishra for his contribution.
2. Sanjeeb Mukherjee, 'Rising Inequality Should Concern Us All, Says Former PM Manmohan Singh', *Business Standard*, 25 June 2019, https://www.business-standard.com/article/economy-policy/rising-in-equality-should-concern-us-all-says-former-pm-manmohan-singh-119062500047_1.html.
3. *Widening Gaps: India Inequality Report 2018*, Oxfam India.
4. Sarah Anderson and John Cavanagh, 'Top 200: The Rise of Global Corporate Power', Global Policy Forum, 2000, https://www.globalpolicy.org/component/content/article/221-transnational-corporations/47211.html.
5. *Widening Gaps: India Inequality Report 2018*, Oxfam India.
6. Ibid, p. 17.
7. Ibid, pp. 10–11.
8. *Widening Gaps: India Inequality Report 2018*, Oxfam India.
9. Ibid.
10. Oxfam India, 'Oxfam Inequality Report: Public Good or Private Wealth?', 2019, p. 3.
11. Jean Drèze and Amartya Sen, *An Uncertain Glory: India and Its Contradictions* (Princeton University Press, 2013).
12. Ibid.
13. Ibid.
14. Sukhadeo Thorat and Nidhi Sadana Sabharwal, 'Addressing the Unequal Burden of Malnutrition', *India Health Beat* 5.5 (2011), http://www.bpni.org/Article/Policy-Note-Number-5.pdf.
15. *Widening Gaps: India Inequality Report 2018*, Oxfam India, p. 50.
16. Barbara Harriss-White and Nandini Gooptu, 'Mapping India's World of Unorganised Labour', *Socialist Register* (2001): 89–118.
17. Sonal Sharma, 'Of Rasoi ka Kaam/Bathroom ka Kaam', *Economic and Political Weekly* 51.7 (2016): 52-61.

18. Sumeet Mhaskar, 'The State of Stigmatized Employment in India: Historical Injustice of Labouring', *Mind the Gap: The State of Employment in India*, Oxfam India, 2019, p. 185.
19. Jean Drèze and Amartya Sen, *An Uncertain Glory: India and Its Contradictions* (Princeton University Press, 2013).
20. *Widening Gaps: India Inequality Report 2018*, Oxfam India, p. 53.
21. Maria Thomas, 'India's Growth Story is Leaving Out Its Muslim Minority', Quartz India, 24 September 2018, https://qz.com/india/1399537/indian-muslims-have-the-least-chances-of-escaping-poverty.
22. Prime Minister's High Level Committee, *Social, Economic and Educational Status of the Muslim Community of India*, Government of India, 2006, p. 150.
23. Maria Thomas, 'India's Growth Story is Leaving Out Its Muslim Minority', Quartz India.
24. *Widening Gaps: India Inequality Report 2018*, Oxfam India, p. 71.
25. Ibid.
26. *Widening Gaps: India Inequality Report 2018*, Oxfam India, p. 35.
27. Development Finance International, 'The Commitment to Reducing Inequality Index 2018: A Global Ranking of Government Based on What They are Doing to Tackle the Gap Between Rich and Poor', Oxfam, 2018, https://s3.amazonaws.com/oxfam-us/www/static/media/files/The_Commitment_to_Reducing_Inequality_Index_2018.pdf.
28. Amitabh Behar, 'Inequality is the Moral Challenge of Our Times. Stop Evading It', *Times of India*, 2 February 2019, https://timesofindia.indiatimes.com/blogs/voices/inequality-is-the-moral-challenge-of-our-times-stop-evading-it.
29. Council for Social Development, *India Social Development Report 2018: Rising Inequality In India* (Oxford University Press, 2018).
30. Himanshu and Abhijit Sen, 'In-Kind Food Transfers-I', *Economic and Political Weekly*, 48.45 (2013).

From Social Democracy to Social Accountability

1. Excerpts from the speech to the Constituent Assembly on 25 November 1949.

2. *Public Good or Private Wealth?* Oxfam Report, 2019.
3. This section borrows excerpts from Rakshita Swamy, *Explorations in the Concept of Social Accountability: from Theory to Practice and from Practice to Theory* (New Delhi: Centre for Budget and Governance Accountability, 2019).
4. Shiksha Samwaads in Kumbhalgarh, Rajasthan were borne out of collective efforts by the local people of Kumbhalgarh, the Mazdoor Kisan Shakti Sangathan (MKSS), the SR Abhiyan and the Centre for Policy Research.
5. *National Campaign Committee for Central Legislation on Construction Labour (NCC-CL) v. Union of India*, https://main.sci.gov.in/supremecourt/2006/17160/17160_2006_Judgement_19-Mar-2018.pdf.

The Right to Education and Health: Is the State Giving Up?

1. Union Budget 2018–19.
2. Data on allocations from Economic Survey 2017-18.
3. Indranil Mukhopadhyay, 'Healthcare at ICU Doors as Government Spend Drops, Again', *Hindu BusinessLine*, 5 February 2017, http://www.thehindubusinessline.com/specials/pulse/healthcareaticu-doorsasgovernmentspenddropsagain/article9522766.ece?css=print.
4. https://pib.gov.in/PressReleaseIframePage.aspx?PRID=1612534
5. Union Budget 2018–19.
6. As of 30 July 2018, Minister of State for HRD Upendra Kushwaha mentioned in the Lok Sabha that there are 9,00,316 vacancies at the elementary level and 1,07,689 posts at the secondary level.
7. Muchkund Dubey, Ashok Pankaj and Susmita Mitra, 'Still Too Many Children Out of School', *The Hindu*, 4 September 2018, https://www.thehindu.com/opinion/op-ed/still-too-many-children-out-of-school/article24857149.ece.
8. Rural Health Statistics, 2018, Ministry of Health and Family Welfare, https://nrhm-mis.nic.in/Pages/RHS2018.aspx?RootFolder=%2FRURAL%20HEALTH%20STATISTICS%2F%28A%29%20RHS%20-%202018&FolderCTID=0x01200057278FD1EC909F429B03E86C7A7C3F31&View={09DDD7F4-80D0-42E3-8969-2307C0D97DDB}.

9. Abinash Dash Choudhury, 'Primary Schools: Merger Muddle', *The Hindu*, 19 July 2019, https://frontline.thehindu.com/cover-story/article28259500.ece.
10. Sulakshana Nandi, Helen Schneider and Samir Garg, 'Assessing Geographical Inequity in Availability of Hospital Services under the State-Funded Universal Health Insurance Scheme in Chhattisgarh State, India, Using a Composite Vulnerability Index', *Global Health Action* 11.1 (2018).
11. Sakthivel Selvaraj, Anup K. Karan and Indranil Mukhopadhyay, 'Publicly-Financed Health Insurance Schemes in India: How Effective Are They in Providing Financial Risk Protection?', in *India: Social Development Report 2014*, ed. Imrana Quadeer (New Delhi: Council for Social Development, 2015).
12. See Indranil Mukhopadhyay and Dipa Sinha, 'Painting a Picture of Ill-health', in *A Quantum Leap in the Wrong Direction?*, ed. Rohit Azad et al. (New Delhi: Orient BlackSwan, 2019) for a detailed discussion.
13. Based on the RTE Forum submission of the Draft NEP 2019.

MGNREGA: A Distress Saviour or a Saviour in Distress?

1. The authors would like to thank Sailasri Kambhatla and Sakina Dhorajiwala for their helpful comments in the initial draft.
2. https://www.youtube.com/watch?v=wi037kOLaP4.
3. http://mospi.nic.in/sites/default/files/publication_reports/Annualpercent20Reportpercent2Cpercent20PLFSpercent202017-18_31052019.pdf?download=1.
4. https://secc.gov.in/welcome.
5. https://sites.google.com/a/iitgn.ac.in/high_resolution_south_asia_drought_monitor/drought-early-warning-system/dews-india. The website provides real-time data and the archived data is available only on request. The authors have the archived data of 2 August 2019.
6. https://economictimes.indiatimes.com/news/economy/indicators/indias-urban-unemployment-rate-slows-in-march-quarter-government-data-reveals/articleshow/72199226.cms?from=mdr.

7. Ishan Anand and Anjana Thampi, 'Most Regular Jobs in India Don't Pay Well: PLFS', Livemint, 6 August 2019, https://www.livemint.com/politics/policy/most-regular-jobs-in-india-don-t-pay-well-plfs-1565075309032.html.

8. http://mnregaweb4.nic.in/netnrega/all_lvl_details_dashboard_new.aspx.

9. http://mnregaweb4.nic.in/netnrega/all_lvl_details_dashboard_new.aspx All data in this paragraph is from the official website.

10. http://mnregaweb4.nic.in/netnrega/all_lvl_details_dashboard_new.aspx.

11. Sonalde Desai, Prem Vashishtha and Omkar Joshi, *Mahatma Gandhi National Rural Employment Guarantee Act: A Catalyst for Rural Transformation* (New Delhi: National Council of Applied Economic Research, 2015).

12. Karthik Muralidharan, Paul Niehaus and Sandip Sukhtankar, *General Equilibrium Effects of (Improving) Public Employment Programs: Experimental Evidence from India* (Cambridge, USA: National Bureau of Economic Research, 2018).

13. Stefan Klonner and Christian Oldiges, *Safety Net for India's Poor or Waste of Public Funds? Poverty and Welfare in the Wake of the World's Largest Job Guarantee Program* (Heidelberg: University of Heidelberg, 2014).

14. Desai, Vashishtha and Joshi, *Mahatma Gandhi National Rural Employment Guarantee Act: A Catalyst for Rural Transformation*, p. 59.

15. Himanshu and Sujata Kundu, 'Rural Wages in India: Recent Trends and Determinants', *Indian Journal of Labour Economics* 59.2 (2016): 217–44.

16. Mehtabul Azam, *The Impact of Indian Job Guarantee Scheme on Labor Market Outcomes: Evidence from a Natural Experiment* (Bonn: Institute for the Study of Labor, 2012).

17. https://www.google.com/url?q=http://www.righttofoodindia.org/data/navjyoti08_employment_guarantee_and_women%27s_empowerment.pdf&sa=D&ust=1581221528668000&usg=AFQjCNHcvWDuhy0yjVtiG9M3cC4iyflXlQ.

18. A Study on 'Socio-economic Empowerment of Women under NREGA' by the National Federation of Indian Women (NFIW)

for the Ministry of Rural Development, Government of India, August 2008.

19. Jagdish Bhagwati and Arvind Panagariya, 'Rejoinder on NREGA', *Times of India*, 19 November 2014, https://timesofindia. indiatimes.com/blogs/toi-edit-hpage/rejoinder-on-nrega.

20. Sudha Narayanan, 'MNREGA and Its Assets', Ideas for India, 15 March 2016, https://www.ideasforindia.in/topics/poverty-inequality/mnrega-and-its-assets.html.

21. Shilp Verma and Tushaar Shah, 'Beyond Digging and Filling Holes: Lessons from Case Studies of Best-Performing MGNREGA Water Assets' (Anand: IWMI-Tata Water Policy Program, 2012), http://www.iwmi.cgiar.org/iwmi-tata/PDFs/2012_Highlight-42.pdf.

22. Anjor Bhaskar and Pankaj Yadav, *All's Well that Ends in a Well: An Economic Evaluation of MGNREGA Wells in Jharkhand* (New Delhi: Institute for Human Development, 2015).

23. Rakesh Tiwari et al., 'MGNREGA for Environmental Service Enhancement and Vulnerability Reduction: Rapid Appraisal in Chitradurga District, Karnataka', *Economic and Political Weekly* 46.20 (2011): 39–47.

24. Tashina Esteves et al., 'Agricultural and Livelihood Vulnerability Reduction through the MGNREGA', *Economic and Political Weekly* 48.52 (2013): 94–103.

25. Sudha Narayanan, *MGNREGA Works and Their Impacts: A Rapid Assessment in Maharashtra* (Mumbai: Indira Gandhi Institute of Development Research, 2014).

26. Anjor Bhaskar, Amod Shah and Sunil Gupta, '7.5 Crore Green Jobs? Assessing the Greenness of MGNREGA Work', *Indian Journal of Labour Economics* 59.3 (2016): 441–61.

27. Rinku Murgai and Martin Ravallion, 'Employment Guarantee in Rural India: What Would It Cost and How Much Would It Reduce Poverty?' *Economic and Political Weekly* 40.31 (2005): 3450–55.

28. http://pib.gov.in/newsite/PrintRelease.aspx?relid=186415.

29. Rajendran Narayanan, Sakina Dhorajiwala and Rajesh Golani, 'Analysis of Payment Delays and Delay Compensation in NREGA: Findings across Ten States for Financial Year 2016–2017', *Indian Journal of Labour Economics* 62.1 (2019): 113–133.

30. https://main.sci.gov.in/supremecourt/2015/41648/41648_2015_Judgement_18-May-2018.pdf.

31. For more details, see Narayanan, Dhorajiwala and Rajesh Golani, 'Analysis of Payment Delays and Delay Compensation in MGNREGA: Findings Across Ten States for Financial Year 2016–2017', *Indian Journal of Labour Economics* 62.1 (2019): 113–33.

32. https://www.downtoearth.org.in/news/agriculture/mnrega-wage-hike-less-than-minimum-wage-in-33-states-63791.

33. *Sanjit Roy v. State of Rajasthan*, https://main.sci.gov.in/jonew/judis/9840.pdf.

34. Rajendran Narayanan and Madhubala Pothula, 'A Triple Blow to Job Guarantee Scheme', *The Hindu*, 16 May 2018, https://www.thehindu.com/opinion/op-ed/a-triple-blow-to-job-guarantee-scheme/article23896197.ece.

35. Ankita Aggarwal, 'Tyranny of MGNREGA's Monitoring System', *Economic and Political Weekly* 52.37 (2017).

36. Sakina Dhorajiwala, 'MGNREGA: Honest Labour's Love Lost As Government Makes Payment Process Complex', *Economic Times*, 25 April 2018, https://economictimes.indiatimes.com/blogs/et-commentary/mgnrega-honest-labours-love-lost-as-government-makes-payment-process-complex.

37. Jean Drèze, 'Done by Aadhaar', *Telegraph*, 3 August 2018, https://www.telegraphindia.com/opinion/done-by-aadhaar/cid/1467855.

38. Debmalya Nandy, 'Aadhaar-Based Payments through the Fragile Rural Banking System Adding to Workers' Sufferings', Sabrang, 15 March 2019, https://sabrangindia.in/article/aadhaar-based-payments-through-fragile-rural-banking-system-adding-workers-sufferings.

39. Kentaro Toyama, *Geek Heresy: Rescuing Social Change from the Cult of Technology* (PublicAffairs, 2015), Chapter 5.

Key to Reducing Inequalities through Accountability, Transparency and Participation

1. Paul Divakar and Beena Pallical, 'The Novel Coronavirus and Its Impact on the Most Marginalised Communities', Amnesty International, April 2020.

2. NewsClick, 'Covid19: Dalit Woman Says She Was Beaten Up, Denied Rations in Saharanpur', https://www.newsclick.in/COVID-19-Dalit-Woman-Beaten-Denied-Rations-Saharanpur.

3. CNN, 'Under India's Caste System, Dalits Are Considered Untouchable. The Coronavirus Is Intensifying That Slur', https://edition.cnn.com/2020/04/15/asia/india-coronavirus-lower-castes-hnk-intl/index.html.

4. Facundo Alvaredo et al., *World Inequality Report 2018* (Paris: World Inequality Database, 2018), https://wir2018.wid.world/files/download/wir2018-summary-english.pdf.

5. Kamal Mitra Chenoy, 'What do Populist Authoritarians Do When They Rule', *Economic and Political Weekly* 54.24 (2019).

6. Katherine S. Newman and Sukhadeo Thorat, 'Caste and Economic Discrimination: Causes, Consequences and Remedies', *Economic and Political Weekly* 42.41 (2007).

7. Times Now, Mirror Now, August 2019, https://www.timesnownews.com/mirror-now/in-focus/article/amendments-in-rti-act-is-a-much-larger-issue-than-we-are-thinking-says-anjali-bhardwaj/462396.

8. John Dayal, Leena Dabiru and Shabnam Hashmi, *Dismantling India: A 4-year Report* (New Delhi: Media House, 2018).

9. *Handbook on Social Welfare Statistics* (New Delhi: Ministry of Social Justice and Empowerment, 2018), http://socialjustice.nic.in/writereaddata/UploadFile/HANDBOOKSocialWelfareStatistice2018.pdf.

10. Wire, 'Most Crimes Against Dalits are Against SC Women: NCRB Data', December 2017, https://thewire.in/caste/ncrb-crimes-against-dalits-women.

11. Newman and Thorat, 'Caste and Economic Discrimination: Causes, Consequences and Remedies'.

12. Press Trust of India, '634 Deaths Related to Manual Scavenging Recorded in 25 Years: NCSK', *Business Standard*, 18 September 2018, https://www.business-standard.com/article/pti-stories/634-deaths-related-to-manual-scavenging-recorded-in-25-years-ncsk-118091801081_1.html.

13. *Scheduled Caste Sub-plan: Guidelines for Implementation* (New Delhi: Planning Commission, 2006).

14. *Dalit Adivasi Budget Analysis 2019–20* (New Delhi: National Campaign on Dalit Human Rights, 2019).

15. This has been excerpted from *Dalit Adivasi Budget Analysis 2019–20* (New Delhi: National Campaign on Dalit Human Rights, 2019),_ http://www.ncdhr.org.in/wp-content/uploads/2019/07/ NCDHR-Budget-2019_Withcut-Mark-Single-1.pdf.

16. For 2015–16 and 2016–17, the due allocations are calculated as per the Jadhav Committee Guidelines issued in 2010. For 2017–18 and 2018–19 in the post-merger of Plan and Non-plan Budgets, the due allocations are calculated as per the budget circular of the respective years. For 2019–20, the due amount has been calculated by the new guideline issued by the finance ministry—No-F.2(21) B(P&A)/2016, Government of India, Ministry of Finance, Department of Economic Affairs, Budget Division, 26 December 2017. This guideline gives the ministry-wise allocation for SCs and has named it as Development Action Plan for Scheduled Castes (DAPSC). As per the guidelines, each obligatory ministry/department is given a set proportion of the CS+CSS to be earmarked as the budget for SC and ST schemes.

17. Ibid.

18. This has been excerpted from *Dalit Adivasi Budget Analysis 2019–20.*

19. Direct fund refers to the allocations which directly benefit SCs or take them out of poverty or reduce the gap between them and the others. It is also seen that schemes developed by many ministries and departments are more in the nature of welfare and not oriented towards economic mobility, skill development, land purchase, employment or enterprise development, which would directly enhance the living standards of SCs. These are only 'paper allocations' where population proportion budgets are reported as SCP allocations and utilizations.

20. This has been excerpted from *Dalit Adivasi Budget Analysis 2019–20.*

21. Under allocation and unspent balances as evidenced in NCDHR's *Dalit Adivasi Budget Analysis 2017–18.*

22. *Dalit Adivasi Budget Analysis 2019–20* (New Delhi: National Campaign on Dalit Human Rights, 2019).

The Role of Independent Institutions in Protecting and Promoting Constitutional Rights

1. https://www.hindustantimes.com/india-news/4-senior-supreme-court-judges-speak-out-against-cji-dipak-misra-say-need-to-preserve-institution-for-survival-of-democracy/story-UqaLGhs4iCbyk4zckVmMbM.html.
2. https://doj.gov.in/sites/default/files/action%20plan.pdf.
3. https://www.barandbench.com/columns/rafale-decision-is-mr-modi-an-imperium-in-imperio.
4. https://indianexpress.com/article/india/sexual-harassment-allegation-against-cji-gogoi-in-affidavit-complainant-alleges-husband-brother-in-law-faced-brunt-5686263.
5. https://www.indiatoday.in/india/story/cji-sexual-harassment-row-retired-justice-cites-institutional-bias-says-woman-must-get-report-1531823-2019-05-22.
6. https://www.thehindu.com/news/national/cji-sexual-harassment-case-have-a-right-to-copy-of-bobde-panel-report-says-complainant/article27059607.ece.
7. *Campaign for Judicial Accountability and Reforms v. Union of India*, https://main.sci.gov.in/supremecourt/2017/34846/34846_2017_Judgement_01-Dec-2017.pdf.
8. There are two existing mechanisms: The In-House Procedure to deal with allegations against judges relating to the discharge of judicial function, or with regard to conduct or behaviour outside court (https://main.sci.gov.in/pdf/cir/2014-12-31_1420006239.pdf) and a Gender Sensitisation and Internal Complaints Committee (GSICC) set up by the Supreme Court.
9. https://www.thehindu.com/news/national/rti-integral-says-supreme-court-but-refuses-to-come-under-it/article26283856.ece.
10. https://www.indiatoday.in/india/story/cji-under-rti-act-but-conditions-apply-supreme-court-in-landmark-order-1618462-2019-11-13.
11. *Supreme Court Advocates-on-Record Association and Another v. Union of India*, https://main.sci.gov.in/jonew/judis/43188.pdf.
12. https://www.livelaw.in/sc-collegiums-biggest-crisis-justice-chelameswar-refuses-attend-meetings.

13. https://www.thehindu.com/news/national/why-delay-appointments-asks-supreme-court/article30845600.ece and https://timesofindia.indiatimes.com/india/sc-raps-govt-over-delay-in-judges-appointment/articleshow/72408432.cms.

14. Refer https://main.sci.gov.in/jonew/judis/29918.pdf.

15. https://www.firstpost.com/india/justice-p-sathasivam-kerala-governor-bad-sign-indian-judiciary-1700995.html.

16. https://www.epw.in/engage/article/right-information-promise-participatory-democracy.

17. *Report Card of Information Commissions in India* (New Delhi: Satark Nagrik Sangathan [SNS] and Centre for Equity Studies [CES], 2018), www.snsindia.org/IC2018.pdf.

18. *Report Card of Information Commissions in India,* SNS & CES, 2019, p. 22, http://snsindia.org/wp-content/uploads/2019/10/Report-Card-2019-FINAL.pdf.

19. *Anjali Bhardwaj and Others v. Union of India and Others*, https://main.sci.gov.in/supremecourt/2018/15968/15968_2018_Judgement_15-Feb-2019.pdf.

20. Timeline given in petition filed to Supreme Court in 2018 (https://www.livelaw.in/centre-states-stifling-functioning-of-rti-act-petition-in-sc-to-fill-vacancies-in-cic-state-commissions).

21. See judgments in *Union of India v. Namit Sharma* [(2013) 10 SCC 359], *Jagte Raho v. The Chief Minister of Gujarat* Writ Petition (P.I.L.) Nos. 143 and 278 of 2014, SLP(C) No(s).30756/2013 order dated 20.04.2017, *Varre Venkateshwarlu and Others v. K. Padmanabhaiah and Others*, *Anjali Bhardwaj and Others v. Union of India and Others* (Writ Petition No. 436 of 2018).

22. *Report Card of Information Commissions in India*, SNS & CES, 2019, p. 8, http://snsindia.org/wp-content/uploads/2019/10/Report-Card-2019-FINAL.pdf.

23. Ibid.

24. *Safeguarding the Right To Information* (New Delhi: RTI Assessment & Analysis Group (RaaG) and National Campaign for People's Right to Information (NCPRI), 2009), http://snsindia.org/wp-content/uploads/2018/10/RAAG-study-executive-summary.pdf; *Peoples' Monitoring of the RTI Regime in India: 2011–13* (New Delhi: RTI Assessment and Advocacy Group (RaaG) and CES, 2014), http://x.

co/raagces; *Tilting the Balance of Power: Adjudicating the RTI Act* (New
Delhi: Research, Assessment and Analysis Group (RaaG), SNS and
Rajpal & Sons, 2017), http://snsindia.org/Adjudicators.pdf; *Tilting
the Balance of Power: Adjudicating the RTI Act*, (New Delhi: RaaG,
SNS & Rajpal, 2017), http://snsindia.org/Adjudicators.pdf) *Report
Card of Information Commissions in India* (New Delhi: SNS & CES,
2018), www.snsindia.org/IC2018.pdf; *Report Card of Information
Commissions in India*, (New Delhi: SNS & CES, 2019), *http://snsindia.
org/wp-content/uploads/2019/10/Report-Card-2019-FINAL.pdf.*
25. Anjali Bhardwaj and Amrita Johri, 'Right to Information:
Dangerous Knowledge', *India Today*, 2 August 2019, https://
www.indiatoday.in/magazine/up-front/story/20190812-right-
to-information-dangerous-knowledge-1576016-2019-08-02.
26. Anjali Bhardwaj and Amrita Johri, 'Undermining the Lokpal',
Economic and Political Weekly 54.18 (4 May 2019), https://www.
epw.in/journal/2019/18/commentary/undermining-lokpal.html.
27. *Common Cause v. Union of India*, https://main.sci.gov.in/jonew/
judis/44826.pdf.
28. *Common Cause v. Ajay Mittal*, Contempt Petition (Civil) no.
714/2018 in Writ Petition (Civil) no. 245/2014.
29. https://www.deccanherald.com/lok-sabha-election-2019/
kharge-not-to-attend-lokpal-selection-panel-meet-723364.html.
30. https://in.reuters.com/article/cbi-supreme-court-parrot-
coal/a-caged-parrot-supreme-court-describes-cbi-
idINDEE94901W20130510.
31. *Vineet Narain and Others v. Union of India and Another*, https://
main.sci.gov.in/jonew/judis/13548.pdf.
32. *Alok Verma v. Union of India*, along with *Common Cause v. Union of India*,
https://main.sci.gov.in/supremecourt/2018/40089/40089_2018_
Judgement_08-Jan-2019.pdf.

Rights-Based Development and Democratic Decentralization in Kerala

1. Swami Vivekananda, 'Future of India', *The Complete Works
of Swami Vivekananda*, Mayawathi Memorial Edition, Vol. 3,
(Kolkata: Adwaithashrama), pp. 294–95.

2. *Government of Kerala Economic Review*, Vol. I (Thiruvananthapuram: Kerala State Planning Board, 2019).
3. Ibid; A.V. Jose, 'Changes in Wages and Earnings of Rural Labor', *Economic and Political Weekly* 48.26 (2013).
4. T.M. Thomas Isaac and Richard W. Franke, *Local Democracy and Development, People's Campaign for Decentralized Planning in Kerala* (New Delhi: Left Word, 2000).
5. The network of women NHGs are known by the name 'Kudumbashree', which literally means 'grace of the family'. There is also a Kudumbashree Mission to provide support to the network. The NHGs are federated at the ward level (ADS) and at the gram panchayat or municipal level (CDS).
6. S.M. Vijayanand, 'People's Participation in Poverty Reduction Programmes: A Case Study of the Integrated Tribal Development Project (ITDP), Attappady', MPhil thesis (Thiruvananthapuram: Centre for Development Studies, 1997).
7. Paulo Freire's book *Pedagogy of the Oppressed* argued that education should allow the oppressed to regain their sense of humanity, which would in turn enable them to overcome their condition.
8. S. Narayanan and Upasak Das, 'Employment Guarantee for Women in India: Evidence on Participation and Rationing in the MGNREGA from the National Sample Survey', *Working paper No. WP-2014-017* (Mumbai: Indira Gandhi Institute of Development Research, 2014).
9. Government of Kerala, *Report of the Expert Group on Total Housing Mission* (Thiruvananthapuram: Kerala State Planning Board, 2016).
10. T.M. Thomas Isaac, Budget speech 2020–21, Government of Kerala, Thiruvananthapuram.
11. Joy Elamon, Richard W. Franke and B. Ekbal, 'Social Movements and Health: Decentralization of Health Services—The Kerala People's Campaign', *International Journal of Health Services* 34.4 (2004); Jos Chathukulam, 'Reflections of Decentralised Health Delivery System in Kerala', *Mainstream* 54.6 (30 January 2016); Jacob John and Megha Jacob, 'Local Governments and the Public Health Delivery System in Kerala: Lessons of Collaborative

Governance' (Newcastle: Cambridge Scholars Publishing, 2016); Azeez 2015.

12. T.M. Thomas Isaac, Budget speech 2020–21, Government of Kerala, Thiruvananthapuram.

13. http://www.kudumbashree.org.

14. Bina Agarwal, 'Can Group Farms Outperform Individual Family Farms? Empirical Insights from India', *World Development* 108 (2018): 57–73; K.P. Kannan, G. Raveendran, *Poverty, Women and Capability: A Study of the Impact of Kerala's Kudumbashree System on Its Members and Their Families* (Thiruvananthapuram: Laurie Baker Centre for Habitat, 2017).

15. Based on direct communication from Dr Joy Elamon, director, Kerala Institute of Local Administration.

16. S.M. Vijayanand, 'Kerala's Management of COVID-19: Key Learnings', Ideas for India, 2 May 2020, https://www.ideasforindia.in/topics/governance/kerala-s-management-of-covid-19-key-learnings.html; T.M. Thomas Isaac, 'Ahead of the COVID Curve', *Indian Express*, 17 April 2020, https://indianexpress.com/article/opinion/columns/coronavirus-covid-19-kerala-curve-6365935.

17. D. Narayana, C.S. Venkiteswaran and M.P. Joseph, *Domestic Migrant Labour in Kerala* (Thiruvananthapuram: Gulati Institute of Finance and Taxation, 2013).

About the Contributors

Prabhat Patnaik is professor emeritus at the Centre for Economic Studies and Planning, Jawaharlal Nehru University. His areas of interest are macroeconomics, political economy and development economics. He is the author of several books, including *Accumulation and Stability under Capitalism, The Value of Money, Re-Envisioning Socialism* and *A Theory of Imperialism* (with Utsa Patnaik).

Jayati Ghosh is professor of economics at Jawaharlal Nehru University, New Delhi. Her research interests include globalization, international trade and finance, employment patterns, macroeconomic policy, gender issues, poverty and inequality. She has authored and/or edited a dozen books and around 200 scholarly articles. Her recent books include *Demonetisation Decoded: A Critique of India's Monetary Experiment* (with C.P. Chandrasekhar and Prabhat Patnaik), *The Elgar Handbook of Alternative Theories of Economic Development* (co-edited with Erik Reinert and Rainer Kattel) and *India and the International Economy*. She has received several national and international prizes, including the M. Adisheshaiah Award for distinguished contributions to the social sciences in India (2015); the International Labour Organisation's Decent Work Research Prize (2010); the NordSud Prize for Social Sciences of the Fondazione Pescarabruzzo, Italy (2010); and the Ava Maiti Award and the Satyendranath Sen Prize from the Asiatic Society, Kolkata.

Amitabh Behar is the CEO of Oxfam India. He is passionate about governance accountability, social and economic equality and citizen participation. Over the years, he has worked on building people-centric campaigns, alliances for social justice and linking micro-activism to macro changes. Amitabh is one of the leading experts of people-centred advocacy and he chairs the organizational boards of Amnesty International India, Navsarjan and Yuva. He is the vice board chair of CIVICUS and also on the board of other organizations like Centre for Budget and Governance Accountability, Mobile Crèche, VANI and the Global Fund for Community Foundation.

Savvy Soumya Misra worked at All India Radio, the *Telegraph*, CNN-IBN and *Down to Earth* magazine before joining Oxfam India in 2014. She found her calling in rural reporting while working at *Down To Earth*. At Oxfam India, for the last five years and more, she has been documenting its work and is currently with the public engagement team. She has published a book to commemorate ten years of Oxfam India called *Beyond Charity*, which contains the stories of Suresho, Chitamma, Birsa and many more.

Paras Banjara is from the nomadic tribal community of Banjaras. He is the first postgraduate from his community in Rajasthan. After finishing his master's in social work, he has donned many roles: a programme officer under MGNREGA in the Rajasthan government, a resource person at the Andhra Pradesh Social Audit Unit and a consultant with the National Commission for Protection of Child Rights, where he promoted people's monitoring of the education system. He has also worked at the Centre for Policy Research on issues concerning the education sector. At present, Paras is with the social accountability and resource unit, and is also associated with Suchna Evam Rojgar Adhikar Abhiyan, a large network of civil society organizations dealing with rights-based issues. He is based in the Kumbhalgarh block of Rajasthan. While he is primarily involved in promoting accountability and transparency in the social sector, he also takes up issues concerning the rights and entitlements of nomadic tribes.

Shankar Singh is one of the founder members of the Mazdoor Kisan Shakti Sangathan. Acknowledged to be one of India's leading figures in people's theatre, he has combined over four decades of activism with the power of people's communication through street theatre, puppetry, song and drama to strengthen the voice of the poor. He is a seminal member of national and state campaigns associated with the right to information, right to work and right to food. He continues to live in and work from Devdungri, Rajasthan, and engages with issues of rights and accountability faced by some of the most marginalized sections of society.

Ambarish Rai is the national convener of the Right to Education Forum, a collective platform of education networks, teachers' organizations and prominent educationists, working towards building people's movements to achieve the goal of equitable and quality education for all children through the Right to Education Act, 2009. He is a champion from India under the Gulmakai Network, the Malala Fund's key initiative to support girls' education. He is also the focal person from India in the Global Consortium on Privatisation in Education and Human Rights and he has been involved in the consultation process for the Abidjan Principles on the human rights obligations of states to provide public education and to regulate private involvement in education. Rai has worked for tribal rights in Gujarat and Maharashtra and on labour and peasants issues in Uttar Pradesh. Previously, as the National Organizer, National Alliance for Fundamental Right to Education, he played a vital role in demanding the Fundamental Right to Education which made education a fundamental right through the 86th constitutional amendment.

Srijita Majumder has been working with the Right to Education Forum since June 2018, engaged in advocacy for the realization of the fundamental right to education of every child. She is also the coordinator of the Girls' Education Initiative at the RTE Forum. She has been part of the development sector for nearly five years now. Majumder has a master's degree in politics with a specialization in international relations from Jawaharlal Nehru University, New Delhi.

Dipa Sinha teaches at the School of Liberal Studies, Ambedkar University, Delhi. She has for long been associated with the Right to Food campaign.

Rajendran Narayanan teaches at Azim Premji University, Bengaluru. He has been actively involved in national campaigns on NREGA and the Right to Food. He is a founder member of an action research group called LibTech India that works with labourers, activists and researchers to improve transparency and accountability and enhance participatory democracy.

Annie Raja is the general secretary of the National Federation of Indian Women. She has been one of the founder members of the People's Action for Employment Guarantee that played a seminal role in the advocacy and campaigning for the passage of the MGNREGA, and is deeply involved in the monitoring of the implementation of its act. She led the first set of social audits on MGNREGA in the country in Kerala. She authored the study on 'Socio-economic Empowerment of Women Under NREGA' supported by the Ministry of Rural Development and the United Nations Development Program. She is a member of the Right to Food campaign that advocates for the protection and promotion of the right to food of citizens. She is also associated with the Communist Party of India as a member of the national executive.

N. Paul Divakar is an advocate for Dalit rights, economic rights expert, and a human rights defender. He is currently the chairperson of the Asia Dalit Rights Forum which works in the South Asia region to ensure inclusion and to address issues of untouchability and caste-based discrimination.

Beena Pallical is currently general secretary of the Dalit Arthik Adhikar Andolan of the National Campaign on Dalit Human Rights. Her main focus continues to be on economic justice and specifically gender equity.

Juno Varghese is national coordinator, research, with the Dalit Arthik Adhikar Andolan and is in charge of research and policy work.

Adikanda Singh is national coordinator, advocacy, with the Dalit Arthik Adhikar Andolan and has been working mostly on ensuring the participation of Dalits in policy formulation and data analytics.

Prashant Bhushan is a senior public interest advocate and human rights activist. He has been a relentless crusader for the rights of the poor and marginalized. He is known for his use of public interest litigation to support a number of causes related to corruption in high places, including judicial corruption, environmental protection and human rights. He is also convenor of the Campaign for Judicial Accountability and Reforms.

Anjali Bhardwaj is co-convenor of the National Campaign for Peoples' Right to Information and a founding member of the Satark Nagrik Sangathan. She has been working extensively on issues of transparency and accountability for over two decades. Bhardwaj has been involved with carrying out research on the implementation of the RTI Act in India and has co-authored several national assessments. She has been closely associated with the Right to Food Campaign in India and is convenor of the National Alliance of Peoples' Movements.

T.M. Thomas Isaac is currently the finance minister in the Kerala government, an office he previously served from 2006–11. He is also a four-time MLA from Alappuzha. He was a professor at the Centre for Development Studies before joining the Kerala State Planning Board as member in charge of decentralized planning. In this capacity, he played a key role in designing and implementing the People's Plan Campaign for decentralized planning. He has authored more than two dozen books in Malayalam and English. His works include *Local Democracy and Development: People's Campaign for Decentralized Planning in Kerala, Democracy at Work in an Indian Industrial Cooperative: The Story of Kerala Dinesh Beedi* (along with Richard W. Franke), *Building Alternatives: The Story of India's Oldest Construction Workers' Cooperative* (along with Michelle Williams) and *Challenges to Indian Fiscal Federalism* (along with R. Mohan and Lekha Chakraborty).

S.M. Vijayanand is a retired IAS officer of the Kerala cadre, batch 1981, and he retired as the chief secretary of Kerala. Prior to that, he served as the secretary, Union Ministry of Panchayati Raj. He steered the seminal People's Plan Campaign of Kerala that led to the decentralization revolution in the state, in the capacity of serving as secretary, local self-government and planning departments in the state. He nurtured the Kerala Institute of Local Administration into an international centre of excellence for capacity building in local governance and decentralized planning, especially for elected representatives. He was also directly involved in setting up and mentoring Kudumbashree, Kerala's SHG programme which has attained wide acclaim in India and abroad. He has been a supporter and mentor of various rights-based campaigns and movements, striving towards a more just and equitable life for all citizens.

About Samruddha Bharat Foundation

Samruddha Bharat Foundation is an independent socio-political organization established after the Dr B.R. Ambedkar International Conference held in July 2017 to:

1. Further India's constitutional promise
2. Forge an alliance of progressive forces
3. Encourage a transformative spirit in Indian politics and society.

Addressing both the symbolic and the substantive, SBF works to shape the polity, serve as a platform for participatory democracy, shape public discourse and deepen engagement with the diaspora.

In doing so, SBF works closely with India's major secular political parties on normative and policy issues. It has also created a praxis between India's foremost academics, activists and policymakers, as well as people's movements, civil society organizations, think tanks and institutions. Finally, it has established Bridge India as a sister organization in the United Kingdom to do similar work with the diaspora.

For further details, see:

www.samruddhabharat.in

 @SBFIndia

 Samruddha Bharat Foundation

 @SBFIndia